ADAMANT

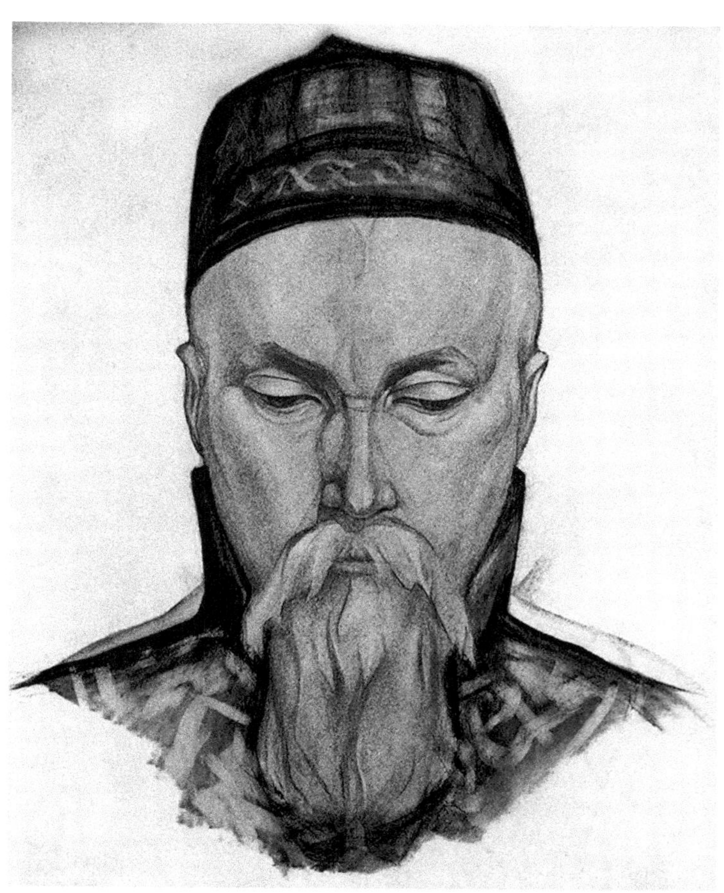

Portrait of Nicholas Roerich by Svetoslav Roerich

ADAMANT

NICHOLAS ROERICH

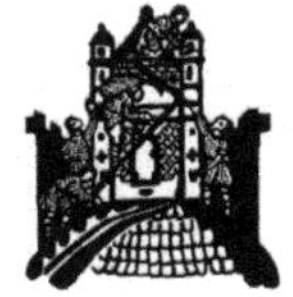

NICHOLAS ROERICH MUSEUM
NEW YORK MMXVII

Nicholas Roerich Museum
319 West 107th Street
New York NY 10025
www.roerich.org

First edition published in 1923. Second edition 2017.

Cover illustration: Nicholas Roerich. *Bridge of Glory*. 1923.

INTRODUCTION TO THE FIRST EDITION

I

PEACE and wisdom through Beauty! Such is the message of Nicholas Roerich, pronounced at the very time when so many are vainly seeking the secret of international peace through suppression, through armament, through hate.

For America, Roerich's gospel has a peculiar significance because within his soul there dwells a profound understanding and love for this country. Some twenty-three years ago in his native Russia he indicated his confidence in our artistic future, by assisting in the first America Art Exhibition in Russia. Since then he has ever been a sincere friend of America. To him, in turn, America has paid its reciprocal tribute, by the profound reverence with which his works have been greeted in this country. Upon his arrival in America for the exhibition of his works in 1920, he was welcomed everywhere and his exhibition which toured America, as well as that of his new paintings in New York, won for him a series of personal tributes. He has been made an honorary member of the Boston Arts Club, Honorary President of Corona Mundi, Inc., Honorary President of the Master Institute of United Arts and has been accorded numerous other honors.

To Russians, the name of Roerich is coupled with such geniuses of their nation as Mussorgsky and Dostoyevsky and his influence during his directorship of the School for the Encouragement of Arts in Petrograd, and as first president of the Mir Iskusstva cannot be overestimated.

Notwithstanding the close relationship which seems to unite him at once to Russia and America, Roerich's influence transcends any single nationality, as evidenced by the fact that the seven hundred of his paintings are distributed through twenty countries. His is a vision without boundaries. His paintings, beside their magnificence, have the quality of prophecy, a quality which one of his countrymen has summed up by saying, "Roerich is capable of seeing further and clearer than the uninitiated. Through the veil of the temporary, he sees the eternal."

And truly Roerich's vision is that of one who reads from scrolls unseen by the neophyte. His spirit has prophesied visions of a new world, where rife and discord are no more, and where the power of Beauty in Action fills mankind with ineffable Love and understanding.

And for this reason a special significance is connected with the following extracts from his letters, which we have the great privilege of publishing in this volume.

Serge Whitman

II

"THE world of Roerich is the World of Truth. His works link mortal souls with the world of unearthly revelations." So said Leonid Andreyeff in the last article before his death. And now as Roerich leaves America for an extended trip to the Orient we realize the surety of Andreyeff's vision. In the short time that Roerich has been in America, his influence in our art life has been tremendous, one that has left a lasting and mature impress on artists throughout the country. The results of his rotary exhibition of two hundred paintings which was seen in twenty-eight cities in America, is felt in a great response from the people and younger artists, who have found in the work of this great man, a new goal towards which to strive. The personal honors and distinctions given to Roerich during his stay are too numerous to cite, but all attest high tribute to the artist. Roerich's monument in this country will be the two institutions which he founded and of which he is honorary president; the Master Institute of United Arts and Corona Mundi Inc. The first of these, one of the greatest departures in the teaching of the arts, promises a new unity among creative workers of the future; while the second provides for the creative artist an outlet for his works, and aims to become the much needed intermediary between public and creator. Already the influence of these institutions is being felt and so rapidly have they grown that a permanent home for them has already been secured. In connection with these Institutions, we find, besides Nicholas Roerich as honorary president, Louis L. Horch as president, Maurice Lichtmann vice-president, Frances R. Grant, executive director and on the faculty are Alfred Bossom, Alberto Bimboni, Claude Bragdon, William Coad, Federic Jacobi, Robert Edmund Jones, Sina Lichtmann, Nicola Montani, Dhan

Gopal Mukerji, Carlos Salzado, Lee Simonson, Albert Sterner, Deems Taylor, and Stark Young and many others of similarly wide international standing. Roerich leaves America assured that his visit has not been in vain, and that the institutions which he founded are already beginning to fulfill their purpose of spreading the international language of Beauty, which he proclaimed as man and artist, and which must open for all the Sacred Gates. And now Roerich is going Asia-wards. The special purposes of his trip are not to be announced for the present, but long since when Roerich was one of those who assisted in the building of the Buddhis Temple in Petrograd, he already revealed his interest in those ancient Teachings. It is also remembered in Russia that the father of Mme Roerich presented the project for the building of the most beautiful synagogue in Petrograd.

In America Roerich has also found inspiration for new paintings and once more as we behold these works, we see again that his vision has penetrated the veil of tomorrow. His paintings, like parables, prophesy the coming of a new world. His spirit, filled with the beauties of yesterday and tomorrow, foresee the fulfillment of the beautiful old legends in this new land of the future: America.

Especially is this prophetic quality seen in his *Sancta* and *Messiah* series. One among these is *The Bridge of Glory* in which is seen the background of Maine, with the Northern Lights at play. And here Roerich has seen Saint Sergius, the most enlightened of all educators, standing before that greatest phenomenon of northern nature, the Aurora Borealis, in exalted meditation about the Bridge of Glory.

And now Roerich sees also the approach of the Messiah amidst American landscape. Is this not verily superb! For in one painting of his *Messiah* Series, we have the Grand Canyon as background. In another the wide-spreading landscape of Arizona is used for this universal subject. The basis of the two works is two old legends, one that the Messiah is coming in a white cloud and that the comet is as a sword in his hand. The old scrolls are coming to flower in the hands of new-world understanding.

So we see in the painting *Legend* that a young man is walking through the typical Arizona landscape with the old scroll in his hand. And behind him the white cloud in the form of a majestic horseman is already appearing, and the comet is flashing as a sword. This painting is entitled *Legend* and is painted in the deep green of early morning.

In another called *Miracle* we have also a most ancient legend which relates that the Messiah shall come across a bridge, and we already see seven figures prostrated before that most transcendent radiance which is approaching the bridge. Certainly the miracle is so great that only part of this powerful aura can be seen. And in the back-ground, as an ancient temple, stand the outlines of the Grand Canyon.

Perhaps this is the first time that America's impelling landscape was used by a foreigner for so exalted and universal an ideal. But can Roerich really be called a foreigner to America? Truly his spirit is international, and so close is he to America that with other countries, we also may claim him as our own.

For Roerich showed his confidence in America's spiritual life before ever he visited its shores, and now in these creations he again attests the prophecy of her spiritual future. For in this young world, amidst the grandeur of America's heights and in ineffable beauty is approaching the Great Unifying Messiah.

M. Highlander

CONTENTS

ADAMANT

ADAMANT

TO the sacred ideals of nations in our days the watchwords, "Art and Knowledge", have been added with special imperativeness. It is just now that something must be said of the particular significance of these great conceptions both for the present time and for the future. I address these words to those whose eyes and ears are not yet filled with the rubbish of everyday life, to those whose hearts have not yet been stopped by the lever of the machine called "mechanical civilization."

Art and Knowledge! Beauty and wisdom! Of the eternal and still renewed meaning of these conceptions it is not necessary to speak. When but starting on the path of life, every child already instinctively understands the value of decoration and knowledge. Only later, under the grimace of disfigured life does this light of the spirit become darkened, while in the kingdom of vulgarity it has no place, and is unknown. Yes, the spirit of the age attains even such monstrosity!

It is not the first time that I have knocked at these gates and I here again appeal to you:

Amongst horrors, in the midst of the struggles and the collisions of the people, the question of knowledge and the question of art are matters of the first importance. Do not be astonished. This is not exaggeration, neither is it a platitude. It is a decided affirmation.

The question of the relativity of human knowledge has always been much argued. But now, when the whole of mankind has felt directly or indirectly the horrors of war, this question has become a vital one. People have not only become accustomed to think, but even to speak without shame about things of which they evidently have not the slightest knowledge. On every hand men repeat opinions which are altogether unfounded. And such judgments bring great harm into the world, an irreparable harm.

We must admit that during the last few years European culture has been shaken to its very foundation. In the pursuit of things, the achievement of which has not yet been opened to mankind, the fundamental steps of ascent have been destroyed. Humanity has tried to lay hold of treasures which it has not deserved and so has rent the benevolent veil of the goddess of Happiness.

Of course, what mankind has not yet attained it is destined to attain in due time, but how much man will have to suffer to atone for the destruction of the forbidden gates! With what labor and with what self-denial shall we have to build up the new bases of culture!

The knowledge which is locked up in libraries or in the brains of the teachers again penetrates but little into contemporary life. Again it fails to give birth to active creative work.

Modern life is filled with the animal demands of the body. We come near to the edge of the terrible magic circle. And the only way of conjuring its dark guardians and escaping from it is through the talisman of true knowledge and beauty.

The time when this will be a necessity is at hand.

Without any false shame, without the contortions of savages, let us confess that we have come very near to barbarism. For confession is already a step towards progress.

It matters not that we still wear European clothes and, following our habit, pronounce special words. But the clothes cover savage impulses and the meaning of the words pronounced, although they are often great, touching, and uniting, is now obscured. The guidance of Knowledge is lost. People have become accustomed to darkness.

More knowledge! More art! There are not enough of these bases in life, which alone can lead us to the golden age of unity.

The more we know, the more clearly we see our ignorance. But if we know nothing at all, then we cannot even know we are ignorant. And that being so, we have no means of advancement and nothing to strive for. And then the dark reign of vulgarity is inevitable. The young generations are not prepared to look boldly, with a bright smile, on the blinding radiance of knowledge and beauty. Whence then is the knowledge of the reality of things to come? Whence then are wise mutual relations to arise? Whence is unity to come, that unity, which is the true guarantee of steady forward movement? Only on the bases of true beauty and of true knowledge can a sincere understanding between the nations be achieved. And the real guide would be the universal language of knowledge and of the beauty of art. Only these guides can establish that kindly outlook which is so necessary for future creative work.

The path of animosity, roughness, and abuse will lead us nowhere. Along that way nothing can be built. Does not a conscience still remain in human nature? The real being in man still seeks to attain justice.

Away with darkness, let us do away with malice and treachery. Mankind has already felt enough of the hand of darkness.

Let me tell you, and mind you, these are not platitudes, not mere words, I give voice to the convinced seeking of the worker: the only bases of life are art and knowledge.

It is just in these hard days of labor, in this time of suffering, that we must steadily recall these kindly guides. And in our hours of trial let us confess to them with all the power of our spirit.

You say: "Life is hard. How can we think of knowledge and beauty if we have nothing to live on?" or "We are far away from knowledge and art; we have important business to attend to first."

But I say: You are right, but you are also wrong. Knowledge and art are not luxuries. Knowledge and art are not idleness. It is time to remember this: They are prayer and the work of the spirit. Do you really think that people pray only when over-fed or after excessive drinking? Or during the time of careless idleness?

No, men pray in the moments of greatest difficulty. So too, is this prayer of the spirit most needful, when one's whole being is shaken and in want of support, and when it seeks for a wise solution. And wherein lies the stronger support? What will make the spirit shine more brightly?

We do not feel hunger or starvation; we do not shiver because of the cold. We tremble because of the vacillation of our spirit; because of distrust, because of unfounded expectations.

Let us remember how often, when working, we have forgotten about food, have left unnoticed the wind, the cold, the heat. Our intent spirit wrapped us in an impenetrable veil.

"The weapon divideth it not, the fire burneth it not, the water corrupteth it not, the wind drieth it not away; for it is indivisible, inconsumable, incorruptible and is not to be dried away; it is eternal, universal, permanent, immovable... Some regard the indwelling spirit as a wonder, whilst some speak and others hear of it with astonishment; but no one realizes it, although he may have heard it described." (*Bhagavad-Gita, Ch. II.*)

Of what does the great wisdom of all ages and all nations speak? It speaks of the human spirit. Penetrate in thought into the deep significance of these words and into the meaning of your life. You know not the limits to the power of the spirit. You do not know over what impassable obstacles your spirit bears you, but some day you shall awake, unharmed and everlastingly regenerated. And when life is hard and weary, and there seems to be no way out, do you not feel that some helper, your own divine spirit, is speeding to your aid? But his path is long and your faint-heartedness is swift. Yet does the helper come, bringing you both the "sword of courage" and the "smile of daring." We have heard of a family which in despair put an end to their lives with fumes of charcoal. Now this was intolerably faint-hearted. When the coming victory of the spirit arrives will not they who have fled without orders, suffer fearfully because they did not apply their labor as they should have applied it? It matters not what labor. The drowning man fights against the flood by all possible means. And if his spirit is strong, then the strength of his body will increase without measure.

But by what means will you call forth your spirit? By what means will you lay bare that which in man is buried under the fragments of his everyday life? Again and again I repeat: by the beauty of art, by the depth of knowledge. In them and in them alone are contained the victorious conjurations of the spirit. And the purified spirit will show you what knowledge is true, what art is real. I am assured that you will be able to call your spirit to your aid. That spirit, your guide, will show you the best paths. It will lead you to joy and victory. But even to victory it will lead you by a lofty path, whose steps are bound together by knowledge and beauty alone... An arduous trial awaits the whole world: the trial by assimilation of truth. After the mediaeval trials by fire, water, and iron, now comes the trial by assimilation of truth. But if the power of the spirit upheld men against fire and iron, then will that same power raise them also up the steps of knowledge and beauty. But this test is more severe than the trials of antiquity. Prepare to achieve! Prepare for that achievement which is a matter of daily life. Meanwhile have care for everything that serves to advance the perception of truth. Approach with special gratitude all that shows forth the stages of beauty. At this time all this is especially difficult.

But adamant-like stands Beauty.

London, 1920.

SHIELD

UNIVERSAL language of the soul is of infinite importance. And it is with special care and tenderness that we should speak the names of those who realize in life that of which we are justly proud.

There are many serious questions before us, but among them the question of the true culture of the spirit will be the cornerstone.

What can replace this spiritual culture? Food and industry are but the body and the digestion. But it is enough for men to reach out temporarily to the body and the digestion while the spiritual life starves. The spiritual level of the nations has sunk. And in the face of all that has happened, in the face of the threatening indubitable return to savagery, any farther sinking of the level will be fatal. In the whole history of mankind neither food nor industry, nor intellect unenlightened by the spirit, have ever built up true culture. And it is with special care that we should treat everything that yet may raise the level of the spirit. I am not dreaming, but asserting.

In every process of reconstruction the level of education and beauty should be raised; in no case should it be forgotten even for a moment. This is not an abstract judgment; on the contrary it is the task before us.

A great period of reconstruction awaits humanity. You of the new generation... apart from all your daily needs, prepare for the achievement of true joyous labor.

In Sweden I said: "We know that Russia has not ceased to be a great country; after enlightened reconstruction on popular principles it will assume a fit place in the sphere of culture, based on its spiritual and natural wealth. We know how incomprehensibly uninformed the West is concerning Russia... even the best of its people: we know with what injurious incorrectness they judge Russian possibilities. But while respecting all the cultural attainments of the East and of the West, we feel that we too can justly set forth truly universal treasures and in them express the cultural physiognomy of the great Russian people. For the language of art and knowledge is the only true and international language, the only language of a firmly established public life. In our internal reconstructions we must, under the benevolent standard of enlightenment, indefatigably introduce beauty and knowledge among the broad masses of people; we must introduce them firmly and actively, remembering that what now lies before is not ideology, not the work of formulating, but work itself, creation—the essence of which is clear and comprehensible, without saying many words about it. Not words but deeds! We must remember that the image of beauty and knowledge will heal the people of slackness of thought, will inspire them with the bases of personal and public resources. It will make plain the essence of work and show the people, in a more comprehensible light, the path to the lofty attainments of the spirit.

"But to attain these simple, basic forms of assimilation the Russian intelligentsia, despite the smallness of its numbers, must show, self-sacrificingly, mutual goodwill, union and respect toward the manifold ways of spiritual searching.

"The intelligentsia must spiritually guard itself against the vulgarity and savagery surrounding it. Out of the fragments and the precious stones lovingly discovered it must build up the Kremlin of a great freedom, lofty beauty, and spiritual knowledge."

Again, we know that the material side of life has treacherously seized on mankind, but we do not conceal the fact that the intelligentsia must seek out the path of achievement.

And here in London it has already been said:

"We must by all means seek to proclaim and widely realize in life the tasks of true art and knowledge, remembering that art and knowledge are the best international language, remembering that the strength of a people lies in its spiritual might, which is reinforced from sources of living water. Recollect the wise popular tale: the spring of dead water, i.e., all that exists only for the body, caused the limbs of the body to be broken in pieces, but the body could only be brought to life again when sprinkled from the spring of living water. Those sacred springs must be laid open for the healing of the world. There are no lookers-on, there are only workers."

We have to speak in plain clear language, as if we were in the open street. Now life is filled with the old banners of political parties, worn out like defaced, useless coins. Now man is forgotten. Human words are plain and clear, but yet plainer and clearer is the universal language of creative effort with all its mysterious conviction.

The young generation has before it the task of bringing art and knowledge into life. Art and knowledge have often existed in life like locked libraries, like pictures turned with their faces to the wall. But the generation of the young must approach this task actively, vitally, in an ideal way; and their work, the simplest everyday work, must be illuminated by searchings and victories. The paths of art in their agelong stratification lie so deep and are so innumerable, and the sources of knowledge are so bottomless! What a life of joyous labor lies before you, you, who are beginning to work!

Beauty and Wisdom! It is the prayer of the spirit that will raise the countries to the level of majesty. And you, young men and women, can demand the opening of these paths by all means. That is your sacred right. But for the realization of this right you yourselves must learn to open your eyes and ears and to distinguish truth from lies. Remember clearly: what is needed is not ideology, but effectual effort.

Iron rusts. Even steel is eaten away and crumbles if

not vitally renewed. So does the human brain ossify, if not allowed to perfect itself indefatigably. And therefore learn to draw near to art and knowledge. These paths are easy later, but difficult in the beginning. Surmount them! And you, young people, have before you one of the most wondrous tasks: to raise the bases of the culture of the spirit; to replace mechanical civilization by the culture of the spirit. Of course you are witnesses to the cosmic process of the destruction of mechanical civilization and to the creation of the foundations of the culture of the spirit. Among national movements the first place will belong to the re-valuation of work, the crown of which is widely-understood creativity and knowledge. Moreover only these two motive powers make up that international language of which feverishly-seeking mankind stands in such need. Creation is the pure prayer of the spirit. Art is the heart of the people. Knowledge is the brain of the people. Only through the heart and through wisdom can mankind arrive at union and mutual understanding. Now to understand is to forgive. The new governments will inscribe on their banners "the prayer of the spirit, art and knowledge", and will understand that he who bears with him the true spirit of national life must not even for a moment forget the achievement of spiritual life. Otherwise the builder will have no path before him and ruin will await him.

You, the young generation, have the right to demand from the governments the opening of the paths of art and knowledge. You must be able to say with clear conscience that even when circumstances were hardest you did not forget those great foundations of life—beauty and wisdom; that you not only remembered them, but according to your powers you realized in your lives this achievement which replaces the joy of destruction by the true joy of creation. And in the consciousness of this lies the guarantee of a brighter future for you. You know that outside of art religion is inaccessible; outside of art the spirit of nationality is far away; outside of art science is dark.

You also know that the achievement of the life of the spirit is not the privilege of hermits and anchorites alone. It may be achieved here, in our midst, in the name of that which is most sacred and nearest to the Great Spirit. And the consciousness of the achievement of life will open out to you new and daily possibilities of creation.

And so now I speak to you, of the young generation, about art and knowledge. I know that you, the knights of the people, the knights of the spirit, will not remain in the city of the dead; you will build up a country which will be bright and most beautiful and full of wisdom. Every word should end not in destruction, but in upbuilding. We know how mighty is creative thought. So now, before undertaking searching, we must speak words which proceed from the best sources: "Put aside all prejudices; think freely!" And all that is thought in the name of beauty and wisdom will be beautiful.

And again I will say unto you: Remember that the time has now come for harmonizing the centers. This condition will be of the first importance in the conflict with "mechanical civilization", which sometimes is erroneously called culture. The spirit, buried under the petty details of everyday life and barbarously ground down is already raising its head. Its wings are growing. O my young friends! Preserve your bright enthusiasm and your eye of goodness.

And we are not alone in our struggle. The great teacher Swami Vivekananda tells us: "Don't you see I am above all a poet?" "That man cannot be truly religious, who has not the faculty of feeling the beauty and grandeur of art." "Non-appreciation of art is crass ignorance."

Rabindranath Tagore finishes his book *What is Art* with these words:

"In Art the person in us is sending its answer to the Supreme Person, who reveals Himself to us in a world of endless beauty across the lightless world of facts."

There is no other way, O friends, now scattered! May my call penetrate to you. Let us join together by the invisible threads of the spirit. I turn to you, I call to you: in the name of Beauty and Wisdom, let us combine for struggle and work.

London, 1920.

PATH OF BLESSING

LIKE bees we gather knowledge. And we pack our load into odd honeycombs. At the expiration of the year we examine our "treasures." But who has managed to slip in so much that is unnecessary? How have we managed to impede our path so much?

Heavy are the things of yesterday! But from the midst of that which is accidental and subject to destruction, like the ashes of last night's fire, there loom always the landmarks of that which is precious to our Spirit. And the Spirit knows them. It is they that lead mankind through all races, through all the circles of achievement. Steps to the temple!

The Lord Christ pointed out the beauty of flowers.

"Verily, verily, Beauty is Brahman. Art is Brahman.

Science is Brahman. Every Glory, every Magnificence, every Greatness, is Brahman."

Thus exclaimed the Hindu saint coming back from the greatest samadhi. A new path of beauty and wisdom shall come.

The best hearts know already: Beauty and Wisdom are not a luxury, not a privilege, but a joy destined for the whole world, at all grades of achievement. The best men already understand that they must not only talk continually about the paths of beauty and wisdom, but they must actively instill them into their own and into the social daily life, all difficulties notwithstanding. They know that an Occidental garment is not yet the sign of a cultured person. They know that in our days—days of deathly conflict between mechanical civilisation and the coming culture of the Spirit—are particularly difficult the paths of beauty and knowledge, are particularly oppressive the onslaughts of black vulgarity. They do not deny the difficulty of the struggle, but beyond it already grow the wings of the liberated Spirit.

You know Nature's best beauties have been created in places where shocks and quakes have occurred. You know the ecstasy when facing rocks, abysses, the picturesque roads of the old lava. You are amazed at the crystals of struggle and at the wrinkles of thought displayed by the coloured strata of the rocks. The convulsions of Cosmos yield an infinite beauty.

Think, how many signs have been manifested. The War has inundated the world with blood. Droughts, floods have disturbed human welfare. Lakes have dried up. The peak of Mont Blanc has crumbled, Famine has revealed its face. How many conventions of a senile race have already been disrupted?

Amidst the ruins of human conventions already arises a new life. Even the most stupid begin to recognise that a good deal of that which is now visible to them is not accidental. A new world is coming—coming before astonished and utterly surprised eyes.

In the new world, in its new temples, a new life will be established, in which art and knowledge will support the throne of Divine Love. The Blessed Ones lead us along these paths. Amidst the monstrous mental accumulations of obsolete frippery, signs of a synthesis, and of the harmony of perfection, are becoming visible.

Learning the future significance of beauty and wisdom, men will understand also the paths of their creation. At present one must think about art in its all-embracing significance. One must sense, and confirm, the highest conductor of the Spirit, the Consoler and Creator.

Consider! Towards the end of the past century old styles became worn out. Life was filled with dead imitations. Works of creative beauty stood isolated. In house furniture, in objects of daily use, in paintings and sculpture, the average level reached the limit of false indifference. Then a reaction took place immediately. But if the imitation of beauty was hideous, the reaction proved as insulting as the imitations were ugly . A hatred was declared for the old. And hatred, as usual, generated malicious impotence. Sputtering the poisonous saliva of decomposition, they rushed into creating new theories. Like clumsy druggists they distributed the sparks of Divinity into flasks and pasted labels upon them. Thus, in place of arrogant indifference, life was filled with all sorts of -ists and -exs and posts. And once more disunity and disintegration reached the limit. And once more the guardians of true art, such as Rodin, Courbet, Puvis, Van Gogh, Gauguin, Degas, Cezanne, stood isolated, while around them went on the hubbub of the crucifixion of beauty. What a subject for Bosch or old Bruegel! Now they were enslaved by the subject; now they looked only for form; now they recognised nothing but colour. Arbitrarily they divided art into higher, decorative, applied, commercial; they distorted the concept of reality; they split the single tree of art; they bent out of shape everything that their convulsive hands were able to catch hold of; they forgot that which rings in every atom of the starry sky; they forgot that before which their blind theories seem miserable patches; they forgot about harmony; they did not wish to know that the time was approaching for the harmonization of the centres; they forgot that the mysterious charm of art—its persuasiveness—lies in the paths of its origination; they forgot that art is created not by the brain but by the heart and by the spirit. The language you speak is that of the place from which you come. Proceed from the sources of the Spirit. In the mysterious, universalizing paths of art there is, verily, that international language which will knit all mankind.

You know. I am not short-sighted. I enjoy even extreme efforts if they bear traces of Beauty, but cold-blooded theories have nothing to do with creations. We need not inventions, but creations.

Art is for all. Everyone will enjoy true art. The greatest harm is to give the masses false and conventional art. The gates of the "sacred source", I insist, must be wide open for everybody, and the light of art will influence numerous hearts with a new love. First this feeling will come unconsciously, but afterwards it will purify human consciousness. And how many young hearts are searching for something real and beautiful? So give it them.

Bring art to the people, where it belongs. We shall have not only the museums, the theatres, the universities, but also public libraries, railway stations, hospitals and even prisons decorated and beautified. Then we shall have no more prisons.

This is not a commonplace; not a truism. This one must emphasise now and clarify with all the powers of one's spirit; for men have altogether forgotten the path of light and creativeness.

The tongue of man—brilliant and powerful in condemnation—has become weak and pale in praise and affirmation.

But even in these false, reactionary paths, art still continues to be prophetic.

But the guides of life create indefatigably. And one may rejoice at the terrifying boundaries of our chaos. So, from under the foam of the storm rises anew the cliff, washed and shining. The creative activity of construction and universalization is nigh. We know this not from predictions. We already see bright signs. Solitary individuals, separated by mountains and oceans, begin to consider the unification of elements, the creative harmony. Thoughts about unity fly over the world. Youth already inscribes Beauty on the escutcheon of its toil.

Cor Ardens[1] recognises art as the universal medium of expression and an evidence of life. It realises the phenomenon that ideals in art manifest themselves simultaneously in all parts of the world, and therefore acknowledges the

1 A new International Society started in Chicago.

creative impulse irrespective of heritage. Art should be created with an honest mind and from genuine necessity. *Cor Ardens* is a concrete move to bring together, at least in spirit, sympathetic isolated individuals.

"We must walk the rising road of grandeur, enthusiasm and achievement with all the powers of our spirit."

The organisation aims:

First: To form a brotherhood of artists which is international.

Second: To hold exhibitions without juries, without prizes and without sales.

Third: To create centres where art and artists of all countries will be welcome.

Fourth: To work for the establishment of universal museums where works donated by members may have a permanent home.

Cor Ardens shall be the emblem as well as the symbol of this brotherhood of artists.

Does not in these words ring the victory of the Spirit? Has not chaos opened the gates of union? Do not physically separated souls begin to understand one another through the language of highest blessing?

O unseen friends! I know you. I know how inhumanly hard it is for you to endure all the conventions of life and not to put out your torch. I know how painfully difficult it is for you to walk under the glances of those who have built life on the dark concept of money. I know you, lonely ones, before the light which seems lonely to you. My young friends! Always young! But there are many sitting before this very light. And those who sit around one light cannot be lonely. And though your hand has not yet felt the hand-pressure, your spirit will for certainty receive the brotherly kiss.

What immense masses have been erected through brotherly efforts. Every effort toward beauty and wisdom is made lighter by the very fact that it passes through the bed of the single source of light—of that light before which the spirit rises in ecstasy while the physical being trembles.

Do not break, do not beat so, poor heart! Once again, after a long interval, wilt thou learn the power to receive and to hold the might which is near.

The baptismal font of art!

Great is the significance of Beauty for the life of the future. The new world is coming.

"Put aside all prejudices—think freely", thus said the Blessed One.

Santa Fe, 1921.

HOMUNCULUS

I KNOW thee, O homunculus![2] It is thou who didst supply us with so many unnecessary things on our journey. It was thou who didst advise us to distrust all that were young and "inexperienced." It was thou who didst put external facts in the place of the facts of spirit and of essentiality. It was thou who didst gild the frames of the pictures. Thou hast penetrated into councils and leagues and hast hidden the search for perfection with the duties of the grave-digger. Thou art working hard. And within thine unseen kingdom flourishes a most noble hatred of mankind.

Yet, for all that thou art small, we have observed thee already. And we have learnt thy ways. Thou fearest the talisman of love. And love cuts the ground from under what thou buildest. The love of creative perfection! Harmony!

Thou dreamest of burying it under worn-out things. Thou thinkest that the flame of love will flicker out. But thou hast forgotten the mysterious property of the flame! It will light any number of torches, nor will it grow any less.

How then canst thou fight? And even shouldst thou penetrate into all the Leagues of the Nations, forget not that behind the nations stands humanity. And here the industrious homunculus shall not attain success. For, after all, humanity, however slowly, is progressing toward harmony.

Does it not seem strange to you, my friends, that even in our days, these days of the extremest turmoil and ter-

---

[2] The symbol of human vulgarity.

ror, it is nevertheless possible to show forth actively such still far-off conceptions as love, goodness, perfection, i.e., all the companions of harmony. Harmony is often misunderstood. Harmony is not an abstract chanting of hymns. Harmony, the harmonisation of the centers, is the manifestation of activity in all its might, in all its clarity and conviction. Apprehending what we want we combine all our centres into one effort and even overcome all the ordinances of destiny. And our spirit knows, better than any, where truth lies. And every one of our actions is judged by the spirit of truth.

And it is this spirit that knows also that love and perfection will be applied in life in the simplicity and clarity of creative work. If the simplicity of expression the clearness of desire corresponds to the immeasurable majesty of the Cosmos then the path will be a true one.

And this Cosmos is not the unattainable one, before which professors can only knit their brows, but that great and simple one which penetrates the whole of our life, building up mountains and setting light to stars on all the countless planes of the universe.

Simplicity is an inevitable quality of harmony. The creative work of the future will be imbued with simplicity. You will not, of course, confuse simplicity with primitiveness, with pretention. The difference here is as great as between a work of art and a print. And often in gilded frames we find mere commercial prints while true art is fluttering on a poster in the wind and snow.

But the spirit, even if in silence, knows which is the print, the banal, and which is joy and creative work.

Silently question your spirit, as you bring every object into your house. Repeating incantations against the homunculus, think why and how you have arrived at the idea of bringing a new guest to your hearth.

Remember that these silent guests may become true friends, but may also become enemies to your home.

In the cognizance of objects lies their harmony. And again, your spirit distinguishes friend from foe.

We know the immutable healings of music and colours. Let us recall the power of song. Let us recall the exaltation experienced in temples, in museums. The house of God! The House of the Great Mystery. Art alone can clothe the Great Mystery with flesh. And the sacrament of the Spirit has only beauty for its base.

Of course you love art. And you would ask me about many things. You want to know what is best for the harmony of the house, easel paintings or photographs? Is it better to fix the surroundings once and for all? Or is there more vitality in the idea obtaining in China and Japan, where every day one new picture is hung upon the wall of the room? No doubt you would inquire as to the correctness of the idea of our modern exhibitions, where behind the appearance of the temple of art lurks the booth of the shop-keeper?

The Master drove the money-changers out of the Temple. The Master knew, of course, that as yet we cannot do without them in our daily life, but it was out of the Temple that He drove them. So is it in matters of art. Buying and selling, of course, must as yet remain. But they must be expelled from the Temple. Let the feast be open; let the shop be open too. But the shop in the Temple and the likeness of the Temple in the shop create internal corruption in those who create and cynicism among those who look on. The sweet savour of the Temple will arrest the gesture even of the bare-faced cynic and the homunculus must flee. Verily, O homunculus, you will have to desert our life after all. Countless youthful hearts request you to depart.

Having purified the principle of remuneration of art, it becomes possible to introduce the latter into the home, to bring into it, as it were, a taper lighted in the Temple. The idea of wall-painting and the precious change of impressions, as in the East, will both find place in it. For the truth is infinite. And every individual case of the affirmation of art is determined by the consciousness of the spirit.

The railway guard assumes that people do nothing but travel. In the mind of the shoe-maker men do nothing but walk. In the conception of the man of today people do nothing but suffer. But in the knowledge of the Blessed men must rejoice.

True, just at this moment joy over art often sounds strange. Much is said about art, and so little art is brought into men's lives. And always excellent excuses and explanations are offered for this. It is always the most convincing circumstances that are to blame. Everything is to blame; no blame attaches only to the "civilised" man who goes to see bullfights or to watch a bout of fisticuffs carried on according to the rules of the Ring. Here both hearts and purses are open.

Question these people as to how much they have done for art. How much art have they brought into their lives? They will only be surprised at the question, and you shall find that the cave-man of the Stone Age holds the advantage over these conquerors of the earth. Nowadays one has to speak of this too.

How is one not to speak of it when at the present time there are Governments which seek to burden the freedom of art with special taxes and thereby put fresh obstacles in the thorny path of beauty. Here again is the work of the homunculus!

And at the same time only ten per cent of the people bring art into their daily lives and know something about it. About 20 per cent only talk about art, without making any application of it. The remaining 70 per cent. generally speaking, do not know, or rather do not now remember, what art is...

But it is better to iterate, even if but mechanically, "good, good, good", than to repeat, even though it be with a grin: "evil evil, evil." This relative principle has been accepted by many. So in this way let us ask ourselves, if only once a week, what have we done for art during the past seven days. Let politicians, too, and Congressmen, clergymen, bankers and businessmen, and all those who pride themselves on their often Sisyphean labours—let them, too, learn this very easy habit. Where men cannot follow the path of the joy of consciousness, there let the pavement of this road be laid. But efforts are necessary. Otherwise our day threatens the work of art with special calamities. Art must flourish and the spiritual call of music must ring out independently of the state of the Stock Exchange and of the meetings of the League of Nations.

One more "non-platitude." Let us confess and remember with shame that which it is verily needful to remember. In the education of children we *still* forget the development of the creative power. First men seek to instil into the child a mass of conventional concepts. First he is taken through a full course of fear. Then the child is acquainted with all the family quarrels. Then he is shown films, those criminal films in which evil is so inventive and brilliant, and good so dull and ungifted. Then the child is given teachers who, unfortunately, being often without any love for their subject, reiterate the deadening letter thereof. Further, the children are shown all the vulgar headlines in the daily press. Next the child is plunged into the sphere of so-called "sport", that its young head may grow accustomed to blows and broken limbs. And this is how the youth's time is first occupied; he is given the most ignoble and perverted formulae. And after that, besmirched and rusted, he may begin creative work.

This is one of the deepest of crimes. Any machine men treat with greater care than they treat a child. Of course—the machine has been paid for with "almighty" money. It may not be allowed to grow dusty or be soiled with dirt. But no money is paid for the children.

We are often astonished by the unexpected character of a child's drawing, by the melody of a child's song, or by the wisdom of a child's reasoning. Where everything is yet open, there things are always beautiful. But afterwards we notice that the child ceases to sing, ceases to draw, and that his reasoning begins to remind one of so-called children's books. The infection of triviality has already sunk into him, and all the symptoms of this horrible disease have become evident. Ennui has made its appearance, a conventional smile, submission to what is disagreeable, finally the fear of loneliness. Something near, some ever-present, guiding principle, has therefore withdrawn, receded.

But you will not drive the children out of the Temple. Are not the most difficult things so very simple? If even a machine suffers from dust and dirt, how destructively must spiritual grime be to the tender young soul. In mortal yearning the little head seeks for light. In mortal pain it feels all the offensiveness of its surroundings. It suffers, weakens, and sometimes lies in the dust for ever. And the creative apparatus runs down and all its wires fall away.

Open in all schools the path to creative effort, to the greatness of art. Replace banality and despondency by joy and seership. Preserve the child from the grimace of life. Give him a bold, happy life, full of activity and bright attainments. Develop the creative instinct from the earliest years of childhood.

Those scourges of humanity, triviality, loneliness and weariness of life, will thus pass by the young soul of him who creates.

Open up the path of blessing.

Santa Fe, 1921.

COLLECTORS

HOW are we to bring art into everyday life? Where are these blessed paths? Perhaps they are inaccessibly difficult? Or they may require countless wealth? Or only spiritual giants may venture along these paths of beauty?

All assurances will be unconvincing. These doubts can be answered only by a page out of real life.

I shall take the portraits of four of my friends. They have all left us now. Only one of them was rich in money, the other three were rich only in the brightness of their spirits.

The rich collector was the Moscow merchant Tretiakoff. There was nothing in his family to dispose him towards art. Rather did that old merchant family look with suspicion on the art it did not understand. But unexpectedly young Tretiakoff was drawn into a new path. And gropingly, guided by personal feeling, he began to collect pictures of the Russian school. He went his way alone, only now and again listening to the advice of some artist friend. And it was not by chance that the now famous Tretiakoff Gallery in Moscow began to come into being. With the true intuition of the picture-lover, Tretiakoff understood that the Government generally filled its museums mostly with official productions, passing over the best work of the artists. And this official physiognomy of the museums could not reflect the evolution of the national school. So has it ever been. So far, I fear, it will be in the future.

Art has always blossomed with an ardent personal urge, which will comprehend and find and preserve and give to the whole nation. And so the merchant Tretiakoff grasped the national task of art. And he found fresh powerful artists and lightened their path. And he preserved their work, surrounding them with pure delight. But he made his joy a national joy, and while still alive gave the whole of his remarkable collection to the city of Moscow. And the task which he had set himself was no small one. He had not simply gathered together a mass of valuable pictures, but made his collection reflect the whole of the Russian school. Everything that was new, brilliant, important came under the eye of Tretiakoff. This taciturn, grey-headed man, in his large fur coat, indefatigably visited all exhibitions, and nothing could hold him when he considered a picture important. He would mount the steep stair leading to the studio of the young beginner in art. He was the first to see a picture finished. He was first at the opening of an exhibition. But he was also first in the possession of the best and most characteristic work.

It came to pass that the prizes given by the highest art institutions were considered as naught compared with the purchase of a picture by Tretiakoff. And the destiny of the beginner in art was decided not by the Academy, but by this sincere and taciturn man. When there was no more room on the walls in his house, Tretiakoff built another beside it. If this was needed it had to be done. And art was not to suffer any loss.

Of course, it may be said that with Tretiakoff's great wealth it was possible to collect on this vast scale. He was able to choose the best and could gather enough to represent the whole of the Russian school in his collection. It was true that his wealth made this scale possible, but the quality of the collection, his love of the work, and his living creative work in the choice itself of pictures and of men—all this was born not from the amount of his means, but from the countless riches of his spirit. Thus did one man, strong in spirit, do infinitely important national work. And now, should the Government seek to have a new Tretiakoff Gallery, it would find itself powerless, for it was the urge of the spirit that created that inimitable combination of beauty.

This is an instance of ideal creativeness within national limits.

Now for another spiritual portrait. Here we have the same power of spiritual urge along with a mighty struggle with means. It was Count Golenishtcheff-Koutousoff, a well-known poet and worker in the sphere of culture and Chamberlain at the Imperial Court. In his case, family traditions were conducive to the development within him of the love of art. His historical knowledge was great, special deep poetic gifts were his.

His collection consisted of pictures of the old Dutch, Flemish and Italian schools. Its fundamental characteristic was not the search for conventional names but the truth shown in wonderful creations. The collector understood that the names of Rembrandt, Rubens, Van Dyck are purely collective names, that only the lowest type of collector seeks in the dark for that which to him is but an empty sound. But a better knowledge of art shows us a countless number of artists engulfed in so-called great names. And the task of the cultured collector is to distinguish among these forgotten names for truth's sake. If on an excellent picture attributed to Rembrandt we find the signature of Karel Fabricius, his pupil, is a fine picture any the worse for that? Or, again, could Van Dyck paint two thousand portraits in one year? Of course not, but he had up to two hundred pupils.

I know how grieved the Count would be to learn that one of his favourite pictures, by an unknown Flemish painter Haselaer, now hangs in the Metropolitan Museum in New York under the name of Joachim Patinir.

In the name of truth, Count Golenishtcheff-Koutouzoff sought to discover the real names of painters and remedied, as far as he could, the sins of mercenary human history. And what loving intimacy breathed from his choice collection. Every picture, too, had been obtained with difficulty, with privation. Every new addition to the collection was greeted with the disapproval of numerous relations who grudged the money spent on it. And money was so scarce. His small Court salary was not enough to live on. And this collector departed this world surrounded by his real friends, his pictures. And he willed that his collection be dispersed to give new joy to new seeking souls.

Golenishtcheff-Koutouzoff was the type of the refined collector, who, working and rejoicind in new beauty and truth, sends it forth again to serve for the ennobling of the human spirit.

Now for the type of a young collector—an instinctive collector from his schooldays. Instead of the joys natural to his age, the boy develops a love for works of art. From childhood, without possessing any personal artistic capacities, he is distinguished by education and developed taste. He is attracted by all that is beautiful. His spirit seeks to rise.

What pleasure it was to pass the time with young Sleptsoff. While yet a pupil of the Imperial Lyceum, he began to collect pictures. His purchases were not chaotic, not accidental. He knew what he was doing. And all the money given the boy by his mother for pleasures was spent on his noble pursuit. And if sometimes he was short of money, his enthusiasm for his general task never suffered from this.

And this general task was a fine one. The boy developed a love for certain very subtly selected painters, and decided to have specimens of each of them in all the periods of their work —to preserve and to hand on to posterity a complete picture of the creative human life of each. The youth dreamt of the future: each painter was to have a separate room and the whole furnishing of the room was to correspond to the character of the art represented in it—the furniture, the embellishment of the walls and ceiling, the character of the lighting and the floor covering. From this we may gather what subtlety of perception lay in that young soul and what deep love and care surrounded each of the artists represented. In these special rooms choice singing and music were to be heard at times. Or suitable passages were to be read aloud. In a word the dream of harmony of the unity of art was to be realised.

It was a joy to hear how a new work of art was selected for the collection. What subtle and truthful considerations were expressed for discovering and bringing out a new and worthy feature in the creative work of an artist. And you could see in this treatment of art no mere fancy, but a real cultural need. And this subtlety of culture infected those surrounding him. Both thought and speech were purified by this bright ascension of the spirit.

Sleptsoff dreamt of handing over his collection to the nation, without any care for his name. But he left us too early to do so. And he left us in an unusual way. He went out for a ride and did not return. He passed over unexpectedly, in the midst of Nature, listening to the harmony of the Cosmos. An enviable passage—a passage to new beautiful labors.

This was the type of a sensitive soul with ingrained feelings of a future harmony and unity.

Now for one more touching type of a collector.

A very poor officer in a line regiment, stationed in a distant provincial town, reaches out to art with all his soul. Depriving himself of many things. Colonel Kratchkovsky, always pleasant in manner, always active, burning with enthusiasm, seeks to gather a collection of specimens of Russian painting. Of course he is unable to collect large pictures. So he collects small pictures—sketches, studies, drawings. But in its essential value his collection becomes a very considerable one. He seeks out the best painters; he understands that often the sketch is more valuable than the picture itself. He seeks to bring out the character of the artist in its most typical features. This is not a buyer of cheap pictures. This is a true collector. And therewithal he himself is often in want of ten roubles (five dollars), so that for him it is a matter of the greatest consequence whether he has to pay ten roubles more or less for a picture. And he asks the painter to let him have the picture and persistently persuades him to accept a lower price.

And his words produce their effect and the sketches are given him. And he would rejoice with the bright joy of a child, and would write enthusiastic letters about his new treasure. How he loved art, and with what lofty meaning he surrounded the conception of true creative work!

In his will he bequeathed the whole of his collection for public use. More than that, he commanded that all his modest property, all that he had in daily use, be sold, and the proceeds applied to the purchase of more works of art which were to be added to his collection.

This is the type of an outwardly unnoticed but deeply important worker for the culture of the future. His example drew the attention of many. And if you could see his letters written from the battlefield! His was a pure soul. Colonel Kratchkovsky left us during the late war.

I might show you many more characters, full of noble seeking in different spheres of art. But even these four types show the level of those cultural aspirations which are so necessary for humanity.

So do things happen; not in dreams, but in real life—sincerely and actively. And such pure labors are accompanied by a smile of joy. How near are the seekings of art to the attainments of the spirit.

It is time to understand, to note and to apply to life these wondrous channels.

And when art has entered actively, irresistibly and simply into all spiritual development of public life, then it will be brought also into the whole of modern life.

And it is through these channels that the true paths of blessing will draw near to every human heart.

Santa Fe, 1921.

HELPERS

"TELL me who your enemies are and I will tell you who you are."

My friends, do you love your enemies?

Learn to be "proud" not of your friends alone, but also of your enemies. It is a pity that you do not love your enemies. You ought to love them. They are such painstaking beings. They work so hard for you. They know more about you than you know yourselves. In their painstaking efforts they ascribe such subtle inventions to you. In their conception you become both all-powerful and omnipresent. And often your enemies help you and your loftiest ideas. And so often do the blows of your enemies forge new and invisible friends for you.

Having finished their "business", your emboldened enemies will take their seats at councils and meetings and will begin to settle your affairs without you. But the creativeness of life will turn all their decisions upside down like Wagner's Mime; these dear foes of yours will not know exactly what they are saying. Afterwards they will come with explanations, but they will still remain your enemies, until they feel the impact of the spark-arrow. Then, becoming impoverished, they also become both cautious and insightful. And then all is as it should be.

Your foes are often angry. Now he who is wroth is already powerless and is dangerous no more. Having exhausted their cries, they seek to crush you with silence, but how pleasant is work amidst silence. Both with their cries and with their silence they profit you. Ah dear foes! if you could sometimes see what a little mannikin it is that sets you at us. Even the rudest hearts would be ashamed of such a guide and ally.

I say nothing about all those cases when open enemies have forced you to look around, to verify your knowledge and to go on with renewed persistence.

Blessed be the enemies!

"But why do you occupy yourselves with your enemies? Are not all your friends enough for you?" you may ask. Of course I am not speaking for myself and, perhaps, not for you either. But I am speaking for the younger generation. It often knows not how to act towards its first enemies, and instead of simply crossing the river, it piles rock upon rock, losing valuable creative time. Yet at every minute someone could be taught and led to rejoice. To rejoice not with money, but with the joy of coming to know new distances.

If the whole world were to rejoice, were it only for a moment, all the dark walls of Jericho would fall instantly. But it is yet a far cry to the joy of the whole world.

Often we learn a thing so thoroughly that should it turn out to be all wrong, we still resist changing our opinion; instead of gaining a third eye, we reject the two we have.

Passing along a forest road, try, having gone ahead of your fellow-traveller, to slip unnoticed into the undergrowth and let him pass ahead. Then you may call to him from behind, but he will only increase his pace and hear your voice before him. For his brain knows that you are ahead.

Why do people never see a blue horse or a green face? Because, notwithstanding what is evidently right, their fettered brain knows what does not exist in reality.

How many disputes about life, religion, knowledge, beauty, have not been brought into being by fettered brains. Bound in the fetters of schools which are prisons.

So do your enemies know so many things absolutely that they will even help the culture of the future. They will help it unexpectedly for themselves.

Have they not resolved to crush you with their "splendid" material attainments and possessions? They have raised the standard of their completed life, their completed race. In the pride of their knowledge of their completeness they have cut all the "unnecessary" wires. What does the poor Spirit matter before the might of warehouses crammed with manufactured goods, even though the goods be rotten? The enemy are already preparing to triumph and to chant hymns in honour of their negation. But a "silly" thing takes places. Someone or other does not want to take their goods. Time is spoiling their stores, which to judge by their appearance, are not fit to lie beside the products of the most ancient epochs. And from behind that heap of rubbish there will arise, victorious and irrefutable, only the creations of the Spirit.

Let us glance at the museums of our planet, say a thousand years hence. What will our descendants find remaining from our days? They who will have long known both atomic energy and the power of harmony. Books and newspapers, paper, woven stuffs—all will have turned to dust; cement and iron will long have become rubbish. All colours will have turned to yellow and gray. Many statues will have fallen to pieces. What is left of our cemeteries will have become beggarly ruins. And alongside this sorrowful picture there will still remain the monoliths of ancient days which have known more than once the meaning of a thousand years.

Many of the works of your enemies will be swept away by time. True, in the battle of purification some of your friends will perish also. But those who understand what harmony is will be preserved. For they know that harmony consists in the correspondence of all parts and all materials. He who knows what he is working for and what he is expressing, will also create the correspondence of his materials. He will understand how to preserve books—the scrolls of knowledge. He will understand that it is absurd to erect a statue of cement or to paint a picture with colours which he knows to be bad and on rotten canvas.

Gradually people will come to understand what must be preserved and how to preserve it. To preserve it as a trace of the spark of divine energy.

But that one may know, one must think, one must create the moments of this exaltation, of this process of learning.

Many people go to church at the end of the week. Many people recall at the end of the week what accounts they have to pay. But very few people think, even once in a week what, during the past seven days, they have given in the sphere of beauty and knowledge. And it is in vain that art knocks at these closed doors. This knocking of the heart disturbs the brain no more than the rattling of the wind. Only the shutters are closed more tightly and silken curtains deny all access to the fresh air.

No one is obliged to love art. The majority of conversations about it are carried on not for love of it, but only because it is proper to do so. Nevertheless, art and knowledge progress.

A gradually increasing electric current gives an increasing light. Then the light blazes with special brilliancy, and, for us, goes out; but the dynamo works with still greater energy. This means that our sight no longer perceives the vibrations of such a tension. But the invisible light keeps growing.

Or a freight train begins to move before your eyes and hides from you a wondrous landscape. The train increases its speed. In the intervals between the cars bits of landscape begin to flash. The train runs at full speed and you seem to see, as it were, through it, the whole continuous landscape. The obstacle of the physical body has vanished.

In the dark we often do not see a growing light. But, for that, if we concentrate we shall again begin to see, through our physical sheath, the true world, in its true movement.

So even now we often are unable to perceive the increased vibrations of cosmic movements. But through the chain of railway trucks we are already beginning to distinguish the mountain peaks to which destiny is bearing us.

We have recalled the contemporary conditions of creative work. We have recalled all the Golgothas of difficulty and the feats of attainment. Of course, the circumstances of art and knowledge in modem life are abnormal. Of course we must know this and remember it every hour. But if all is moved by creative love, by the miracle of beauty and the wisdom of action, you will be unable to overthrow this triangle, for each side of it shows the other two.

And now, it we know that the young generation remembers the might of these pillars, it will, of course, carry the consciousness of this through all the difficulties of life. And when we speak of brotherhood, love, harmony, we are not repeating absurd, unbefitting, old-fashioned words, but words pertaining to the immediate practice of life. A miracle is being performed in the midst of life, in the midst of action, amidst intense harmony. The visions of night are being transformed not into fables, but into phenomena of happy communication with the paths of the Blessed.

The window opened into the darkness will bring us the voices of the night, but the call of love will bring the answer of the Beloved.

A new world is coming.

Santa Fe, 1921.

SPECTACLE

IT seems especially fitting that in this hall of the Master Institute of United Arts, I should be speaking to you of the Moscow Art Theatre. For the meaning of the words "united Art" was defined in its most exalted sense in the work of the Moscow Art Theater. So all institutions dedicated to United Arts are especially near to that organization.

Everywhere in Russia the name of the Moscow Art Theater has been associated with an atmosphere entirely its own. Never was the name pronounced lightly, but always with a sincere and profound reverence, and not only was this so in the big cities, but even in the smallest villages wherever the fame of the Moscow Art Theater penetrated. When you came to the Theater with its silent, subdued audience, bereft of all gaudy ornament and glaring light, you instinctively felt that you were participating in something serious, something of true art. Nor was this atmosphere brought about through advertisement, or through special efforts, but only through devoted labor.

When for instance, one heard the report from behind the stage, that after the fiftieth rehearsal of a play, complete changes in the production were made, no one was astonished. Certainly, for the average European theater, it would be considered ridiculous to change a complete work after so many rehearsals—in fact it is rare that so many rehearsals have ever been heard in the average Theater. But when we heard this from the Moscow Art Theater, no one was ever surprised. Because, not only in every rehearsal of the Moscow Art Theater was outlined the dead letter of the play, but every rehearsal was a new creative achievement. And so, the creative power was ever increasing. And herein is found the key to understanding the special atmosphere which was the Moscow Art Theater.

It was in 1912 that I came intimately to know the workings of the Theater, for that year, the heads of the organization came to me and asked me in what works I would care to co-operate with them. At first two possibilities were discussed *Princess Maleine* of Maeterlinck, and that cosmic Norwegian drama of Ibsen, *Peer Gynt.* To choose which should be the first, was for me a difficult task, because I so sincerely appreciated the picturesque surface and deep inner side of Maeterlinck. But the pan-human voices of Ibsen's creations were also very close to me, so I finally decided upon the second.

When the Moscow Art Theater sets itself a task—long before the material side of the production is sketched out—the entire subject is studied intensively. And this is done, not only in the libraries, but if some local geographical or historical atmosphere is needed, actors and producers are sent to the very spot to study the subject in the most intimate way. So it was with *Peer Gynt.* When we decided upon this drama, the first question from their side to me was whether I had been in Norway. I answered that I had not. To this they replied, "Then you must go and study all conditions." When I refused, they insisted, assuring me that all accommodation would be reserved and my trip arranged entirely. However. I explained to them that it was always my method first to create the settings and scene, and then perhaps, after, I would go to Norway, because it was always my intention to create my settings from my inner vision, taking the inner sources of the creative work of the author or composer and not to confuse this with local "realities." Finally they agreed to my point of view, but all the principal actors during their summer vacation were sent to Norway and Sweden and, at the very source of inspiration of the play, studied all the circumstances of the drama. In the Autumn, when we discussed my sketches for the drama, my own viewpoint was justified, because, they, coming directly from Norway, admitted that my Norway was the real one.

For the first time, perhaps, it was planned to perform the entire drama with its fifteen scenes. Certainly, not one setting could be repeated, and we had to have about 300 designs for costumes, as the first condition was to have complete variety for every act. Often, because of this attention to detail, the Moscow Art Theater has been accused of being to realistic. But I think that this realism is not the superficial realism of the last century: Maeterlinck's plays are also realistic, but no one accuses them of cheap realism. So, also with the Moscow Art Theater. There, productions are not realistic, but "real"; and certainly one may agree that the finest fairy tale in the world is real life. And it is this fairy tale that is translated by the Moscow players, not only in picturesque productions such as *Tsar Feodor, Julius Caesar* and *Hamlet*, but even in the plays of Russian life by Chekhov, where you have not the superficial intimacy, but the real tragedy of life.

So we began the work, spending innumerable evenings discussing the scheme and characteristic detail of the Ibsen drama.

During these discussions one could discern the real individuality of each personality connected with the theater. One could perceive the skeptical humor of Stanislawsky, the reticent silence of Nemirovitsch-Dantchenko, the quick-Caucasian blood of Marjanoff, the stage-director. After the discussions I was asked, "But what artists will you need to produce your sketches?" Knowing that they were ready to give the finest possibilities for the work, I mentioned several of the best artists and asked them to choose which one of them they preferred. "Why one, if you like all?" was the question. "We shall distribute the work, giving each artist the type of work which is nearest to him." So I received five splendid assistants, each of them getting the finest possible studio, and allowed enough time to complete his work in the finest way. And when some misunderstanding arose about the work I was always invited from Petrograd to discuss and prevent any possible mistake. Thus the work was really a mutual undertaking.

When all the settings were ready and we tried them on the scenes, we were urged to cut out four entirely completed scenes because otherwise the production would have been too long. But do not imagine that there was any disagreement about this; even the shortening of the play was creative, because it was not produced on a paper plan, but through the actual working out of an idea. For only in such a manner can one test in full consciousness what is most effective and expressive for the whole idea. And so with complete mutual understanding, we took out everything that seemed too long or too heavy for the performance.

The same thing happened regarding the actors and personnel. Actors were chosen for the characters after long detailed discussions and yet even up to the fiftieth rehearsal no one had the feeling of completeness. We, of course, used the music of Grieg, and the conductor and composer of the Moscow Art Theater, (who by the way, composed impressive music for *Hamlet* and *The Blue Bird*) arranged Grieg's suite in the finest way. When one realizes how long it took to arrange the undersea music, the scene of Asa's death; how much effort was expended in arranging the music accompanying specific moments of the underwater scene, by using the power of sound in its subtlest nuances, we may understand why so many women had tears in their eyes. The music of the trolls' cave, Solveig's scene and the dance of Anitra, so familiar, became for the public quite new music, because it was given in an entirely new aspect and in a truly living form.

Of course one must not imagine that so complicated a work of united arts is accomplished without labor, and is always calm and smiling. I remember that sometimes Anitra tried out some new steps with tears in her eyes; it is not so easy to change and search for new expression without weariness. Sometimes the faces of the principals were so severe, and the remarks of Nemirovitch-Dantchenko so abrupt and significant, that I, as a stranger, thought that a break was near, and I could not imagine how they could possibly continue the work the next day. But when tomorrow came, every member was ready with new strength and ideas, and new possibilities. Sometimes an actor or actress would come to me and say. "Really, I can do no more. For everything that I did yesterday seems not to be a true representation of the character, but too commonplace. I screamed—but it was too superficial, I must find some other means of expression." And certainly, when you feel you must have another expression, you will find it. It was such a joy to take part in a real work, which though not easy, enlisted true mental endeavor. When we came upon some detail to be worked out, such as, for instance, the storm and wreck of the ship, it was thought out with enough concentrated effort and attention to the minute that the result was realistic enough to cause sea-sickness. Then, for instance, we tried innumerable ways for the black figure to appear from the wall, and finally it appeared quite naturally from the overcoat of Peer Gynt, the illusion being heightened by the realistic tumult of the shipwreck. Yes, this co-operation was real joy.

I would certainly have wished that many costumers and hairdressers could see the attention expended on the costumes and hair-dressing of even the most minor roles. When one realizes this close planning of each detail, one understands why the first day of the performances of the Moscow Art Theater was always the easiest, for everything was in its right place and during that day nothing had to be done: everything was completed and presented with ease.

And now you can understand why the audience at the Moscow Art Theater was so silent and serious during a performance, and why the influence of the production was not that of a theatrical thing, but of a highly educational event, and one filled with the real joy of Art. And it is because of this that in all questions of the resurrection of Russia and of her future, the meaning of the work of the Moscow Theater will be immensely important. We have had many imitators of this theater and many smaller enterprises rose with the same feeling,—but the real traditions of this theater could not be imitated. For these are strongly individual and cannot be repeated.

I am indeed glad that the Moscow Art Theater is coming to America. You have seen many sides of Russian art in America, but this fundamental side must also be known to you. For in that coming union of Russia and America, which I believe in so strongly, it will be necessary for America to know Russia from all its different sides, and to discern behind the colorful theatrical surface, the deep devotion to creative work.

New York, 1922.

SPIRITUAL GARMENT

THE brilliant pageants of the nations have passed before our mental vision, and each of these passing wanderers has in the course of the centuries been adding his mite to the treasure trove of civilisation. Numberless are the nations that have marched on, and toiling and struggling, brought us their offerings. But the treasure-store of humanity is not filled. And among sacrifices without number, through the bewildering maze of cloth, stone and metal, the genuine features of Man are still only dimly outlined in the shadows.

How much urgent work awaits all of us?

One idea, however, has already taken root in our mind: We now understand that all the details of the life we see about us have not been the work of mere accident. They are all full of meaning accumulated in the course of the centuries. If every word, and every letter of our name, has its own significance, and if each step of our existence has its cause and effect, with what rapt attention ought we to regard every manifestation of the great creative process!

Some already realize clearly, while others are only beginning to suspect, as if in a dream, that an intricate process of creative work is going on all around them, and that some forces which they do not comprehend are busy shaping the final forms and aspects of a new life. And how infinite is the complexity of these forces. What seeming trifles often change completely the entire structure of our existence.

Why do men feel satisfied with life under one form of society? And why in different circumstances, do they easily lose their peace of mind, sink into a state of despair, and feel absolutely incapable of creating anything successfully?

How many fascinating riddles and bright speculations! And how many obscure and ignorant answers and conclusions!

Experience, however, is now added to the riddle, and experience is made lucid by knowledge. Men begin to realize that the confines of the actual world are broad beyond our vision. They begin to see that ideas of so-called "mysticism" are most often nothing but the results of downright ignorance. And he who denies the profound reality of all that exists in life is just as benighted as he who would deny the existence of the wireless telegraph, radium, telephotography, and all those perfectly real scientific discoveries which but yesterday seemed mere fairy tales.

Smitten with self-conceit and stupidity, some people are ready to deny all that their little brain refuses to grasp today, all that their ear fails to hear. But time was when the possibility of the discovery of America, too, was denied. It is not necessary to cite here examples of all the numerous varieties of ignorance.

Life, however, goes forward. Little by little, people begin to understand the meaning of "reality." They come to realize that life is full of splendid possibilities, often undiscovered, more often forgotten; and frequently already revealed in symbols which, to the barbarous mind of modern, so-called "civilized" Man, seem childish or barbarous stylizations. And yet we remember that every line of an old ornament is filled with the significance of centuries. And still we feel that each harmonious scheme of color produces in us a certain state of feeling which I may perhaps define as "overpowering" or healing.

The majestic force of color! Men who have before their eyes all the radiant hues of the eternal sky, are deliberately blindfolding themselves, so as to shut out from their vision, the joy that could have long been theirs. And yet, having put on every kind of gray, yellow and smoked glasses, Man's intellect still attempts to penetrate the veil and to witness the power of color. Our own age is beginning to remember the relation existing between music and color.

We are now beginning to introduce colored light schemes in the churches, to concentrate the minds of the worshippers. We are beginning to heal the sick by color. Timidly and hesitatingly, there is coming into life something which rightly ought to proclaim itself boldly. Something which in the spiritual visions of the future is bound to bring new joy to cheerless humanity.

Men are the flowers of God. But does it not seem strange that the garden of these flowers should at present cover the earth with such a black, mournful shroud! Even the most festively-attired crowd covers the face of the earth as if with a stream of dark, gray lava. And, like lava, it destroys all vestige of joy in its path.

It may be that life will succeed in establishing at last the harmony which might be worthy of modern civilisation. And yet, even in the era of the Italian Renaissance the crowd knew how to mingle with the flowers in the fields without smothering them with ink! How, then, are we to remedy this evil? Shall we perhaps dot the somber field of the multitude with bright splashes of color? But then, even an ox is maddened by an unexpected flash of glaring color. And, if we continue our comparison of the crowd with a field of flowers, we will recollect that even the brightest floral designs of nature never offend our eyes, for cosmic creation is always harmonious. The manifestations of this work of nature may even blind our feeble eyesight, by their dazzling power, but they will never be found to give offence.

The question, however, is: How shall we rise from the low level of our present feeble vision to the nobler heights where the cosmic truth shall be revealed to us? We have perhaps forever, or for a long time to come, lost the way to truth and light. It may be that only under most extraordinary conditions of life will our eyes be opened. Or will it be necessary perhaps to change our life completely in order to be purified?

Such are the questions which all of us with trepidation

are asking ourselves in the stillness of the night. Shall the gates of light and truth remain closed to us for ever?

Still, at the same time our spirit keeps telling us that there is nothing barred, nothing forbidden. Our inner voice is whispering incessantly, "Everything is near at hand, all must be true and practicable", and the rejuvenation of our life, too, must be simple; it must begin here, among ourselves, for the spirit of Man—this bridge that leads us to all that is noble and inspiring—never forsakes us.

But where are the tokens? Have we perhaps been forsaken, after all? Are we not being misled?

I do not have to tell you in the present address how innumerable are the wonderful possibilities open to the genius of Man. Let me point out here only one instance.

You have all heard, of course, about the auras which may often be distinguished from each other even by the human eye.

You also know that these auras vary in accordance with our spiritual achievements. And every single thought of ours is capable of either darkening or brightening our aura. Thus every man carries with him, as it were, the thermometer of his spiritual achievements. In the images of the Saints we observe halos; these are merely a portrayal of the auras common to all humanity, and they are particularly distinct in the case of highly spiritual organisms.

Of course, the subject of color auras has always been looked upon as belonging to the province of "mysticism." Even theologians have been speaking rather uncertainly about the halos of the Saints. But here again humanity understood that everything ought to be true and practicable, and again, men discovered a means to the aura in a mechanical way. Nowadays you may go to any scientific institution and, together with your X-Ray picture, obtain a photograph of your individual aura. Not to mention the fact that some people are able to see your aura with the naked eye.

Yes, you will ask, but what has all this to do with the

problem of costume? Very much, indeed! It has a tremendous and direct bearing on the subject.

When you grasp the significance and the meaning of the human color aura, you will understand what color means to our life; and you will then know what color harmony means. And not only will you understand, but you will feel how near at hand may be found one more remedy, and a most simple one, to cure the ills of contemporary life.

One more "secret" of Nature will then be revealed to you, just as easily as the practical meaning of the elements which surround us may be made plain to our senses.

Everything should give us joy. Everything ought to be so simple! And woman, above all, is destined to bring into the world the joys of the near future!

Having learned to know, having become practical, you can understand the causes of your sympathetic as well as antipathetic attitude towards men and things. Consciously and carefully you will then utter the word "harmony." And this alone is sufficient to pave the way for your coming enlightenment.

Once our spirit has come to know a thing, you may rest assured that it then becomes merely a matter of time for our brain to assimilate the still novel consciousness.

Man wears an eternal color dress around his spirit. Man himself, by his thoughts, paints this precious dress with colors of his own choice. He seeks some kind of harmonious relation between himself and his environment. He realizes, of course, that a vivid and powerful combination of colors is far more effective than the scared, moribund color of the mouse. The color of the fading twilight of extinction! You will then realize and feel how powerful is the influence of color in your life. By your own best aura you will attract the best hues of other irradiation. And the best colors of external objects will indirectly help your spiritual raiment to shine forth still more brilliantly. In short, everything ought to be a linking and coupling of mutual help.

Mankind has already learned to know the significance of both the dark and the light magic of the sign—the magic of the line. The majority of ancient ornaments show traces of blessed lines. For this reason the source of these stratifications is often a very blessed one. Now humanity is mastering the forces of color. This is why the problem of dress and costume has, apart from external beauty, also a deep intrinsic meaning. And we have already agreed that such expressions as “I like it”, “It fits me”, or “It gives me pleasure”, may have a deep and necessary significance. All our life is full of these great signs.

You will then find that your room, which appeared to be empty until then, begins to fill, not with apparitions, but with a multitude of necessary and beautiful things. And, like a warrior, you will arm yourself with these objects, for the sake of the blessing which each one of us should bring to the world.

Should anybody smile at this, having failed as yet to grasp the hidden meaning of these words, let him now smile; later he will smile at his own lack of understanding.

Beauty and Harmony are knocking at the door.

Chicago, 1921.

TRUTH

WITH our growing understanding of true realities, we begin to comprehend how conventional are many of the so-called "records of our knowledge." Sometimes even the greatest historical events must be accepted only with due discretion. For instance, the first pages of Russian history open with an account of how three brothers, Rurik, Sinaeus and Truwor, Varengian princes, were invited by the Slavs to rule them. Often men wondered over the strange fact that Rurik had left his heirs while the legendary brothers were entirely wiped out of history. But if we go to Scandinavian chronicles, we shall find that to Russia came the Viking, Rurik *"med sin huus und tru ver"*, meaning that Rurik came with his household and trusted guard. Thus one sees how the historical fact about Rurik's coming with his family and entrusted guard was distorted by the translator into very strange personal names, unfamiliar either in Russian or Scandinavian. In a similar way sometimes even the truth must be searchingly corroborated.

Everyone appreciates the *Song of Songs* of Solomon, and from the popular conception everyone knows that it was written by Solomon himself. There have even been some mythical stories and romances later woven around a poetical Sulamith. But if one carefully examines the real sources, one shall discover that the *Song of Songs* was a beautiful official hymn written by a court singer and addressed to an Egyptian Princess; even such commentators as Origen and Jerome confirm this assertion. Thus in this search for truth one sees that beauty is not thereby desecrated.

Similar discrepancies occur about rulers in the endless

history of our planet. Sometimes we are confronted with quite opposing characters when we compare the conventional sources of a ruler's career with the original roots of the story. Take for instance, the official conception of the great Akbar, and compare it with the highest conception given by a more scientific but less known chronicler. Hence, how much discrimination must be projected, not for the destruction but for the purification of the truth.

Often it is the legend which is confirmed by facts. For instance one can cite the following example. When you are going through the wonderful fairyland of the Indian pueblos in America; when you hear the wonderful songs and profound ceremonial dances; when you examine the household and the everyday utensils of Indian life; when you regard their feet bound in white linen, and the peculiar headdress and ornamented shirts; and when, finally, you see the rich fantasy of the totem poles, then, you have the feeling that you are somewhere in western Russia or Siberia, if you know these lands. Seldom in quite different continents, under quite different circumstances of life, do such striking similarities arise. Thus, this one visible evidence strengthens the old legend that several Indian tribes migrated from Siberia to Alaska. And one can appreciate that this legend is so real and so simple that nothing can be said against it, especially when you see the aborigines.

Last year during my journey to Santa Fe, Dr. Hewitt, director of the Santa Fe Museum, wanted to have some of my paintings on exhibition. With special purpose I promised to give him a real Russian painting; and I gave him one which has for its subject a sacred dance around some old Russian idols, some details of which I took from real Russian excavations. Later I realised how well my purpose had worked out, for during the exhibition I was asked many times if I had been somewhere in Alaska or in the Indian pueblos, because this subject, so characteristic of East Russia or Siberia, was found to be very similar to the subject of life among the American Indians. And the old idol of Russia was constantly compared to the Alaskan totem pole.

I am not well-versed in linguistic matters, but I think that even in language some peculiar reminiscences could be found between the two continents. As an artist, however, I can assert that pictorial and musical similarities tell me quite definitely that this old legend is not an invention of fantasy but an odd fragment of truth. And how many fragments of truth, so simple and so near to us, are forgotten and misunderstood!

Now, at this time of the re-evaluation of our old standards, we must take up fearlessly the revision of our official scientific sources. Certainly, this must be with the one condition that we shall eschew prejudice. Prejudice, one of our most dangerous enemies in life, must be destroyed with all the power of the spirit. And only then quite easily the fragments of truth can be woven together into a new and wonderful texture. And this carpet shall help us to fly from the real past to the real future, and we shall realise that even the legendary flying carpets no longer belong to fairy tales alone but to life. Verily, a wonder tale of all life can be easily manifested to our average human brain if it be directed without prejudice.

Another example regarding prejudice is before my eyes. Not only in workmanship, but even in beauty are we sowing prejudice by going to the limits of specialization. A strange aspect indeed is this of art, when the painter can remain ignorant of music and the musician be silent before a statue. Thus in the Master Institute of United Arts, New York, when we pronounced some unifying words about the different branches of art we were confronted by shock and surprise, that any useful and vital connection should exist between the different branches of art. And yet already in the most natural way, by casting out prejudice and facing the matter without hypocrisy we already see that this unity of arts is not only an ideal matter, but that it can also be used in our daily life, in that very life where to-day so many crimes are committed and so many deplorable brutalities and hypocrisies show themselves.

Thus from many aspects of our life, we may find numberless examples of the same sort. Every sincere artist, and every sincere scientist can give you many worthy assertions of this. And this searching for truth in the face of conventionalism, of hypocrisy, must be the watchword of our days; for already we see a real new generation arising, ready not only for struggle but for victory. Only truth! Only results!

Now we must expose another of our greatest prejudices. In a recent serious article we found the following prejudiced classification: "Education, Sociology, Politics, Religion, Science (including Medicine). Art, Technology." One may well ask why technology is not science. Or why sociology and politics are placed before religion. And, finally, why the place of Art is between medicine and technology.

This position of art must be discussed, because only prejudice can place Beauty with technology. The place of art has frequently been misunderstood. It has even been written that Art is but a secondary manifestation of Divinity. If it means professional skillfulness, certainly it is not secondary, but a still lower manifestation.

But Trismegist Beauty—the all embracing, all creative, all convincing power—must be placed on the right plane. Without exaggeration we can assert the significance of Beauty. We must feel that the Great Teacher will come not only in Love and Truth, but radiant with Beauty. In Beauty alone are all the diverse spirits united.

The strings of Earth reach Heaven only in the rhythms of Beauty. And from the Heights was the command of vital Beauty given. High and glorious is the bridge of Beauty. Miraculous achievements can be inhaled in stepping upon its arches. But one can traverse it only free from prejudice.

New York, 1922.

RHYTHM OF LIFE

LET us concern ourselves with something purely educational. The facts of life give us the best bases to formulate a real educational system. For instance, how significant is the following story: During the season of 1913 in Paris, when the *Sacre du Printemps* was first produced, Mr.Stravinsky and I had a very illuminating experience. I had given the subject for the ballet, taking it from the life of prehistoric Slavs. The spectacular side of the production was no more striking or daring than had been that of *Prince Igor* which was so deeply appreciated by the Parisian public. In the costumes and landscape there was nothing incomprehensible; nor was the music—which now is certainly well-known—at all offensive. In the dance of Nijinsky there were some exotic groups but also nothing too bizarre.

Yet even before the first production we already noticed that Mr. Diaghileff and Astruc, the manager, were somewhat disturbed, as if they expected something. And then during the opening night came one of the biggest scandals. The public whistled and clamoured in such a demonstrative way that really I do not believe they could have heard the music. And the culmination came in the second act when the premiere danseuse appeared alone. Really I admired her courage because she danced not with music but with the accompaniment of a horrible uproar from the entire audience, and the few attempts at applause were drowned amidst the disturbance. *Sacre du Printemps* was given several times that season and always with the same clamour, although the seats were always filled. In fact I, personally, heard several perfectly-attired women, as they entered their box, ask each other, "Do you know when the uproar begins?"

Should anyone ask me what the reason was for this terrific protest, I must sincerely profess my ignorance. To me it remains one of the great mysteries. Further, when the same *Sacre du Printemps* was given two years later, it was not only applauded but unanimously praised. And since then, of course, everyone knows the unanimous praise given to this ballet in Paris and elsewhere. When public opinion changes in a century one can understand that a new generation is at hand. But when in two years, you have the same generation thus changing its attitude towards the same, unchanged work, one can see how, within a short period, the standard of evolving events was entirely upset.

But this unexpected change of mind was certainly not a mystery. It was only that specific rhythm of the coming global change in values.

Just now I cannot recall the title of a very interesting book in which was traced from ancient days, a graph of this scientific line of events and we can see with what feverish speed events have followed each other through recent history. Certainly we should be proud to be on the very top of this whirlwind, taking our lessons from history and retaining for the future our educational experience.

Upon this basis, what type of teacher can we imagine for the near future?—and in this I speak of all arts, for they are all in the same position.

You have two types of teachers—the one teacher knows and affirms; the other knows as much but he is always searching. Only a short time ago many institutions were opposed to the searching teacher because the standard of life was not yet crystallized. But now the crystal of our standard is formed, and we cannot create the next step of life. You perceive that everyone recognizes that this cold crystallized standard is a hindrance, and humanity is ready for a real search.

I observed in the Master Institute of United Arts a very

interesting class given by Robert Edmond Jones, on Theatre Decoration, and his plan of working with the pupils and the sight not merely of dumb individuals but of real co-workers, gave me the impression of the old Italian and Dutch studios where the pupils participated in all the efforts of the master. And I dream of the day when the musician will approach this activity and when a group of such active students can create something really vital.

At present, very often, the theatres and recitals are only the hospitals of music; music itself is not entering the homes, although—strangely enough—every house has its musical instrument. The children repeat the same old studies, but rare is the case when one may hear the young souls trying to express themselves in improvisation, in the beginning of composition. And should they try to do so, how many parents, relatives and even teachers oppose these efforts. They believe that such improvisation will spoil the technique and perhaps even hurt the brain, but in what way otherwise can we traverse the bridge between technique and self-expression? So often does the human soul desire to sing, and so often does it desire to sing something peculiarly its own, some new combination corresponding to its particular mood. And why should it be that the young painter can and must express himself in composition from the very beginning of his instruction, while the singer and musician must suppress these mediums of self-expression? I am not a musician but I know what a deep significance music has had in my life, even though it did not reveal to me the subject given by the composer but revealed itself to my inner being quite differently.

Now, it is essential in education that the young generation quite distinctly must and will search. It is the prohibition of this search that has led to the idea of the destruction of everything old, because everything old is connected in the young mind with what is prohibited. But if we open the door of beauty, not through denying and suppressing, but by showing the real practical way of searching, we shall impart to the young soul a new feeling. Everything must be permitted and only one certificate of honors should exist—the certificate of real culture.

The time of extremism, of revolts against all forbidden mysteries, seems to me passing. If we take the new composers, the most gifted ones, we no longer notice the apparent striving only for the extreme, only for disruption, but instead there is a new desire for something really dynamic, for the combining of rhythm with our inner life. Take Prokofieff, I do not feel in his music extravagance, but some cosmic values; similarly do I appreciate, among the Americans, the same broadness in Carpenter, Deems Taylor, Frederick Jacobi, Emerson Whithorne and Griffes.

After his recent lecture in the Master Institute of United Arts, Ernest Bloch, the composer, spoke to me of the dark forces that we must overcome in our personal and professional life. Certainly, this is true, as well as everything which Mr. Bloch said during his lecture concerning the misunderstanding of rhythm, the lack of constructiveness, all of which is so relevant to the efforts of the artists of our times. But Golgotha for some reasons exists, and every musician, every artist, from the greatest composer to the most modest teacher, has to undertake the same hard work to combine the real rhythm of life with their creations. If we were now in an age like the last civilization of Rome or Byzantium, certainly we would be unable to find this harmonized rhythm, and we would stand unbalanced on one foot. But if we are at the beginning of a new era, if we feel that our time is the time for the fulfillment of gigantic plans, certainly this consonance in rhythm shall be found. Everything weak shall perish; but everything with true force shall be able to express itself with dignity.

There is one way that we have before us: it is the way of the open window, of the open door, when the most precious prana shall come to us. And this remedy is so near. And the young generation is growing. The rhythm of life. Only let us be able to distinguish the sacred rhythm of life—for this law of rhythm acts in the same constructive way as the law of the boomerang—everything is returned. So how careful must we be in the sending!

New York, 1922.

ACTIVITY

IT is said that once the great Akbar drew a line and demanded of his wise man, Birbal, that he shorten the line without cutting or erasing from either side. The latter drew a longer line parallel to it and Akbar's line was thereby shortened. Wisdom lies in drawing the longer line.

When one sees in our day the apotheosis of rush, sometimes we feel helpless to shorten this turmoil, this useless prodigality of forces and possibilities. And only in imagining a longer line of real activity can we decrease the effervescence of the present—the standard of Hurry.

Certainly one must remember: Silence acts; speech gives the impulse to action. Silence compels, speech persuades. The immense and inscrutable processes of the world all perfect themselves within, in a deep and august silence, masked in a noisy and misleading surface of sound. The greatest exertions are made with the breath inhaled, the faster the breathing the greater the dissipation of energy. He who in action can cease from breathing—naturally, spontaneously—is the master of the world energy, the energy that acts and creates throughout the universe.

But there are two kinds of stillness—the helpless stillness of inertia which manifests dissolution and the stillness of assured sovereignty which commands the harmony of life. It is the sovereign stillness which is the calm of the ruler. The more complete the calm the mightier the power, the greater the force in action.

In this calm, true knowledge comes. The thoughts of men are a mesh of truth and falsehood. True perception is marred by false perception; true imagination distorted by false imagination; true memory clouded by false memory. The superficial activity of the mind must cease and a silence succeed the restlessness—then in that calm, in that voiceless stillness, illumination comes upon the mind. And right knowledge becomes the infallible source of right action.

This true activity, invisible to the eyes of rushing crowds manifests itself only in results. And through results one sees with one's physical eyes how much longer the line of activity is, compared with that of Rush.

And the day of Rush is the night of Activity. For nothing is created in rush; perhaps money. But in all history only Croesus was mentioned for his wealth, and even he ended his life pitifully.

To be capable of true action in the midst of bustle, to be capable of silence, stillness, illuminated passivity, is to be fit for "Immortality." The "inaction" of power creates, preserves, and destroys. This action is dynamic with the direct, stupendous driving power of a great natural force.

Even moving wheels at their greatest speed seem unmoving. The harmony of the highest action is not to be distinguished by a physical eye; only the results are apparent.

The real stillness sometimes is covered by a ripple of talk and some minor activity—like the ocean with its lively surface of waves. But it has nothing in common with rush. Rush has some special attribute—for it is always accompanied by vulgarity. You are sure to find during the rush, all aspects of this hideous disease of modern humanity. What is the driving force behind the search of the best of humanity? What is driving the bloody revolutions and the searches for new heroic paths? The human spirit is fighting in all those diverse battles against vulgarity.

When the crowd becomes a mob, what happens? There spreads the black kingdom of vulgarity. To the doors of vulgarity the mob rushes. The same miraculous transformation of the crowd into a mob is seen in the rush for trains, in the rush to meetings, in shopping and in the rush of selling, or the rush of disaster. The same rush, we sometimes discern in music, in colors, in the line of a design, in the rhythm of sculpture.

Shall you now ask what the psychological moment is? Everyone now knows the psychological moment when this paroxysm is growing. One aspect of rush is inevitable. The expression of each eye changes. During the sad performances of rush you never perceive a happy face. Rush is proclaiming feverishly, "go, go, go", and everything obeying this command will hasten away; but the shield of activity is "Come, come." And everything following this call is approaching, multiplying the possibilities. People are too busy. They do not wait for a union of souls and in a brief moment something can occur; the best-mannered crowd can be converted into a mob losing all discrimination, full of the wildest instincts. We have many explanations of this moment, but the most definite one is that vulgarity is becoming predominant.

The realm of this mysterious power of vulgarity is immense. The same vulgarity is bewildering the crowds; it is gilding the frames; it is carving hymns into "Jazz"; transfiguring athletics into cruelties; manifesting the standard of superficial life. Even lips are colored alike.

It is as though the human skin were cast off and animals leapt before one's astonished eyes. But, nevertheless, take human beings into nature. Only take them away from the rush and real human aspects shall arise again. Like a chemical solution!

In the same scientific way, humanity must distinguish rush from activity.

"All forms of tyranny have their beginning in kindness", is a saying all too true. "All forms of vulgarity have their beginning in compromise." One day the smallest compromise. Another day a small compromise, and then suddenly a high priest of vulgarity.

This is not a commonplace, not a truism. We must repeat it now, for much of real activity, much of discrimination will be needed in the near future. And in each movement peoples must distinguish where the vulgar rush is, and where eternal activity.

Practical we must always be. Will constant denunciation repel the darkness? Only bring light in—and darkness never was. So only the negative, criticising, discouraging process will not help.

But the first possibility exists of shortening the line of rush with the comparison of the longer one of activity. Only results!

You can never conquer vulgarity through the power of ugliness. In the power of Beauty lies your victory. Verily, only Beauty can overcome vulgarity and stop the wild rush before the gates of that false, gilded realm. And the victory is not far! Everything that we sometimes call "fallen" has it not also "risen"?

New York, 1923.

WATCH TOWERS OF AMERICA

NOW, on the eve of my departure for a trip to the Orient, I feel I must take the opportunity to tell about my impressions of America and American art. I feel that this privilege is mine because some twenty-three years ago I already had faith in the art of America and assisted in showing an American art exhibition for the first time in Russia. And now I am fully justified in my optimism.

First, I must speak of my opinion of America in general.

I often heard America spoken of as purely materialistic. But every man finds what he most searches for. Every man measures the world from his mental point of view. Life is complicated. We are often blind and deaf to the real miracles of life surrounding us. What is reality? What is fantasy? The people, in their mental blindness, often confuse these conceptions. Like a polished diamond, life reflects light in various ways. Very often where we see the shimmer of red materialistic rays, close to it appears the blue and violet. It is a mistake to assume that the predominant color of a diamond is green or red. If I look at America from the red spot of materialistic Wall Street, America naturally is seemingly only materialistic. But my interest has been in the blue and violet rays of your national life. I found them in abundance and they thrilled me. If you consider closely American life, which has nothing in common with the stock exchange or the street, you will be astonished at the revelations. One finds nowhere, for instance, as many creeds and churches next to each other. This is a clear proof of spirituality. When you attend meetings of any denomination you will find crowded halls. The people do not go there for materialistic reasons. They go there for the call of the soul. People are attracted to the teachings of Blavatsky, Vivekananda, Tagore and other great ones. This country gave birth to Emerson and Walt Whitman; they grew up here and found an echo here. These phenomena are naturally hidden from the masses that rush along Broadway and clamor for the mechanical inventions of life. The mechanical side, however, has nothing to do with the spiritual side that thrives in the shadow of elevators and steam shovels.

Here Claude Bragdon speaks to you about the fourth dimension and about the color organ. Dr.Debey thrills you with the deep science of the horoscope. Dr. Hille shall show you a whole universe in one-thousandth of a drop of liquid gold. You will hear Vedanta and Bahai teachers. You will hear men openly discussing here the union of religions and nations, of moon people and Atlantis. Here you will find people interested in astrology and cosmic consciousness. This is all that same America, which is considered mad for money. The country is great and young,—great and young are its aspirations.

Besides all that we see, we cannot forget the great inventors that are at the same time great poets. Edison, the inventor, is at the same time Edison, the poet; Carnegie, the great manufacturer, was also Carnegie, the great poet; it requires a visionary mind to accomplish what those men have accomplished.

Pointing out the spiritual issues of American life, I cannot ignore its cosmic nature. In America a new nation is being composed by means of a quick experiment of mixing the elements of the world. In our very presence is being formed a new social product, a new national soul which already has the qualities of its inherent ethnic importance. Of all the world's recent projects, this is the most marvelous experiment. Its reality produces realistic ideas of the unions of religions and other universal achievements by means of a future spiritual culture. We know that spiritual culture will ultimately conquer the mechanical civilization. We know that the spirit of man leads evolution and is gaining impetus with every day.

In Russia (and union between America and a future Russia is imminent) exists a beautiful legend of a Sunken City, which will emerge again when the proper time has arrived. Who knows, perhaps, the tops of the towers of that Sunken City are rising and becoming visible? Intensive life, with spiritual roots, deep-buried and healthy, although not always apparent, must produce a strong and varied art. One of the strongest impressions, when I first came here in 1920, was made upon me by such men as Rockwell Kent, George Bellows, Ryder, John Sargent, Davies, Maurice Stern, Ufer, R. Chanler Sloane, Manship, Lachaise, Speicker, Melchers, Prendergast, Freseke, Kroll, and Sterner. Among the younger men I found Faggi, Davey, Johnson, Weisenborn, Hoeckner, Shiva. In the theatrical field, Jones, Urban and Geddes were brought to my attention. All these gave me my first impression of the full variety of the American groups. Several artistic groups are national in feeling, but if this feeling has, in the background, an international viewpoint, they are justified, because America has so many treasures that can be expressed in a truly inspired national feeling.

If you take the poesy of the skyscraper; if you regard the romanticism of the national parks or the profound tragedy and beauty of the Indian pueblos; or again, the somber note of the Spanish relics here, you have so many beautiful things to express that you can understand why the modern American feeling is against repeating the formulas of other countries, but aims to express the original beauties of their own immense land. In this way, to seek original sources, I traveled through America, I visited the beauties of your Middle West plains; through the national parks of New Mexico and Arizona; through Niagara and the Pacific cities. I could perceive what a real future this country has.

During the same travels, it is true, I saw many young artists in difficult situations. It is perhaps hard to say this, yet only through Golgothas is achievement tempered. But I could perceive that America had really many souls devoted to art who, living through the hardest experience, do not surrender their living vision. So I feel that, thanks to the artists, America's creative work is rapidly advancing, and portends to make America a real art center.

Not so happy, however, is the state here with art collectors. If I was fortunate in meeting so many prominent artists, I did not have the same fortune meeting collectors. I met throughout the whole country only a few of them. I met several buyers of art, but the real, sincere collectors I met rarely. In several cities I even found that the distinction between buyer and collector was not realized. Similarly, I found a certain attitude, that it was not good taste to have too many art objects in one home. From where comes this unfortunate tale? I do not know, nor am I eager to know, because life itself will erase this foolish prejudice.

The lack of collectors for me was still more unusual because in Russia we have not so many buyers, but many collectors. In one of my recent articles, I spoke about Russian collectors, giving four portraits of prominent types, one a wealthy business man; another a high official; third, a young student of the University; and fourth, a Colonel in the army. The last one was very poor personally and even in this situation, he found it possible to gather a very precious collection of the first small sketches for paintings, because certainly he was unable to purchase expensive paintings. In such a variety of conditions, and in such a diversity of classes and possibilities, only one thing was unanimous,—the search for Beauty, the desire to have within the home real friends,—objects of art, and originals, because even the smallest original has more significance than a copy.

But this state of devotion to art will also come in America very soon. I have seen here many gifted and inspired teachers in art. Just now I recall a class given in the Master Institute of United Arts by Robert Edmond Jones, and I see what real creative work these prominent artists are inspiring in their pupils. During my travels in America I met a large group of people really devoted to art. Several are directors of museums such as Harshe, Eggers, Laurvick, Mrs. Sage-Quinton, Maurice Bloch, Burrows, Dudley Crafts Watson, Edgar Hewett, Kursworth, and numerous others. They are struggling for art and I can see how from those hospitals of art—the museums—the rays of art will penetrate into everyday life.

Already it seems a truism to speak about the real international language of art. But as a prayer, we must repeat it, because only by severe persistence can we act with full conviction. First, the physician must admonish, "Try the remedy once, and you will see the real results."

New York, 1923.

BEAUTY–THE CONQUEROR

FROM former days, perhaps the fifteenth century in Russia, there has come down to us a legend in which Christ is proclaimed as the highest guardian of beauty. According to this legend, when Christ was ascending to heaven, some troubadours approached Him and asked, "Lord Christ, why are you leaving us? How can we exist without you?" And Christ answered, "My children, I shall give you golden mountains and silver rivers and beautiful gardens and you shall be nourished and happy." But then St. John approached Christ and said, "Oh Lord, give them not golden mountains and silver rivers. They do not know how to guard them, and someone rich and powerful will attack them and take away the golden mountains. Give them only your name and your beautiful songs, and give the command that all those who appreciate the songs and who care for and guard the singers shall have the gates to Paradise open." And Christ replied. "Yes, I will give them, not golden mountains, but my songs; and all who appreciate them shall find open the gates to Paradise."

Herein you have the essential and vital combination of religion and beauty, and you see that the highest symbol of religion becomes the highest guardian of beauty.

Again we have a quotation from the oldest Russian historical chronicle by the Monk Nestor, indicating how Prince Jaroslav appreciated knowledge and beauty: "Jaroslav founded Kiev the Great and its golden gates. Loving the laws of beauty and of the church, and being a master in books, he read them by day and by night and wrote them too, thus sowing in the hearts of true men the love of the written word, which we now reap. But books and images are rivers that carry wisdom through the world and are as deep as rivers. Also Jaroslav lovingly beautified the churches with images and with splendid gold and silver vessels and his heart rejoiced in it."

Besides we have also beautiful quotations from some later chronicles of the fifteenth and sixteenth centuries, teaching us that the best spiritual achievement for rulers is to guard art and even to use art in their own life.

Knowing these quotations, one is not surprised to see in the opera *Snegourotchka* that the Tsar is at the same time an artist, and is beautifying his own palace. This is not merely a sophisticated message for royalty, but also the real belief of the people. For if you ask me what pass you would have to show to be allowed to enter a Russian village, I would give you the best advice: enter the village singing, and the more pleasing your song the better your welcome. If they ask you for a certificate, show them a drawing or a painting; it is the best understood certificate, and you may be assured that you can remain there for ever. You have your shield and your guard.

I am far from proclaiming this solely about the Russian peasant; it is in reality a pan-human feeling. Certainly when you are approaching an American farm, the same countersign and certificate are the best. This is not merely a theory, for I have seen everywhere many farmers and I have that feeling about them. For the heart unspoiled by the turmoil of the cities and nourished upon the beauties from the source of Nature is the same human heart, and is speaking the same pan-human language.

When *Corona Mundi*[3] requested that for their founding statement I give them a quotation, I chose the following from my lecture *Beauty and Wisdom*: "Humanity is facing coming events of cosmic greatness. Humanity already realises that all occurrences are not accidental. The time for the construction of future culture is at hand. Before our eyes the re-evaluation of values is being witnessed. Amidst

[3] International Art Center, New York.

the ruins of valueless banknotes, mankind has found the real value of the world's significance. The values of great art are victoriously traversing all earthly storms. Even the "earthly" people already understand the vital importance of active beauty. And when we proclaim: Love, Beauty and Action, we know verily that we pronounce the formula of the international language, and this formula which now belongs to the museum and the theater must enter everyday life. The sign of beauty will open all sacred gates. Beneath the sign of beauty we walk joyfully. With beauty we conquer. Through beauty we pray. In beauty we are united. And now we affirm these words: not on the snowy heights, but amidst the turmoil of the city—and realising the path of true reality we greet with a happy smile the future."

And now you see that I use this quotation not as an idealist's dream, but for practical life. Those who are not blind must see that the question of art has now become not a matter of some special education, but, as everyone acknowledges, the question of beauty has become the most vital factor of life. Formerly one heard stories of artists dying of hunger while the rich financiers built their palaces. Today, events have brought out the reverse: I have heard stories of bankers dying on the top of mountains of worthless banknotes. And we have already heard how an entire country could be supported by the price of old tapestries. So you see how practically this great evolution is working before our eyes. Besides this another question of the same deep significance is coming into our life. Some days ago a prominent architect told me that he regrets so much not having the constant co-operation of painters and sculptors from the beginning of a project, because, only through this essential collaboration from the very beginning can something really harmonious result. I have often heard dancers say they needed to know something of sculpture and the fluidity of form, and certainly you have often heard that painters require music and that music evokes the significance of colour. In the Master Institute of United Arts I have gained significant experience in this direction, showing how much it is necessary to combine under one roof the idea that the unity of arts is also not far from life, and how all musicians, painters, sculptors, architects and dramatists can be united and supported by each other. For different branches of art do not distress the mind, but stimulate some new center of the brain not yet utilised. And certainly we know how many centers of the brain are left dormant.

The gates of Paradise mentioned in the old legend are not only imaginary, and really the present is the most important time, when the vital medium of art is entering home life. For humanity, distressed by political intrigues and seeing about it the refuse of its old beliefs, is realising how easily this new emotion, constructive and vital, is to be found in daily life.

We have mentioned in the statement of purpose of the Master Institute that even prisons must be beautified, and this is not an allegory. The great prison of life is so easily beautified, and a real key to happiness and joy is to be found: the passport of song and the certificate of painted works. And finally, if we have seen the beautiful evolution of civilisation and culture, so in the same way we can understand how a much more beautiful higher evolution awaits us. And it is near. And it is vital. And it is practical for everybody.

And should someone ask why, in the melee of our days, you can be concerned with questions of art, you may safely answer, 'I know my way'. Friends, if we realise how vital Beauty was during ancient times, what immense use of the emanations of Beauty we can make in our everyday life. If in the Middle Ages Beauty was considered the "Gates to Paradise", and if even a modest old chronicler of the eleventh century could assert his joy before Beauty, how necessary it is now to take all practical advantage of this basis of life, and to repeat as a prayer each day: Love, Beauty and Action.

How all-embracing is Love; how profoundly must be

felt the sense of Beauty, and how vitally must we understand the meaning of that virile expression, Action. And this command must not be forgotten once we introduce it into our daily life. The new era is not far off, and not one day can be lost. Perhaps you will ask me why we must repeat constantly this prayer of Love and Beauty? Because, frankly, so many even of our sisters and brothers try to avoid Beauty in their everyday life, and erroneously they think they have sufficient reason for this mistake. But if Beauty is the Shield of the World, if the aura of the World's Teacher is luminously radiant, even the smallest seeds of this splendour must be reflected in our life. And the awaiting ones and the expectant ones must be the first to prepare the place of Beauty in life. So, vitally, until we see the results, we must repeat this prayer of Beauty—the Crown of Action and Love.

New York, 1923.

STANDARD OF BEAUTY

IF we become shortsighted, we are not alarmed. We go to a physician and through spectacles, find a help for our sight. If someone becomes far-sighted, he is not presumed to be abnormal or supernatural. This is not true of clairvoyance. Yet it seems that if the principle of far-sightedness is understood, it is not difficult to apply the same principle to all other qualities of vision. But here enters the work of prejudice. Instead of recognizing the miraculous power of nature, people are ready to presume some magic, some sorcery—so deep is the power of prejudice even in our so-called scientist.

In the same way, should someone very ancient and very wise pronounce the easy clear word, Clairvoyance, with our inmost feelings, we recognize that a true understanding of this easy expression is possible to every clever human being. It is only obscured by the dirt of several of our centers. It seems that, as in the case of poor sight, we must also call upon the physicians to clear the dust from our brain, and to take measures for helping our vision. But again, prejudices are deep. Their vulgar gesture is beckoning us towards the way of conventional lassitude. It is so easy to conventionally quote some great name, or also conventionally to take our opinion from some pretentious volume. After all, for the human being it is a difficult effort to try some new experience.

However, the thorough understanding of the idea of reincarnation will help us in our earthly life. Amidst our many experiences, the experience of the power of beauty is most exalting to our normal powers. Many times have we repeated that only through the bridge of beauty can we reach the beautiful fires of the opposite shore predestined for us. We have tried to persuade the cowards to overcome the customs of the dark ages and again to use beauty vitally in their daily life.

Now we must consider what we shall take as the basis for judgment about beauty. From ancient times to the present, many canons and rules of beauty have been established. We could distinguish quite decided types of beauty, but as soon as a new type was established, humanity rushed forward to search for another new one. So it should be. Because through superficial rules, through calculation, you cannot establish a sense of harmony. We know that for ascension, cleverness and goodness alone are not sufficient, but spirituality also is needed. Through this creative spirituality we can grasp the rhythm of harmony. Only through this quality can we feel the real creative power.

The common term "intuition" is already within the bounds of spirituality. Therefore we can take as our formula for the judgment of beauty, "through intuition, upon the basis of many personal experiences without any conventionalities or prejudices."

In the wide variations in individuality, in the understanding of art, the quoted formula will always save us from uncertainty. The ignorant, the ungifted, the feeble ones and the wrathful, will very often try to stir up one's judgment. They understand that in this mixing up of standards, they are saving themselves. With the most grandiose and fluent expressions they insist that their judgment is right, but one may easily see how petty and partial it is. And so, we must try to escape from these narrow confines of our present conditions.

Spirituality always leads us to a clear decision, but how to put it on a strong basis in order to destroy the small nests of prejudice? One feels that there are as many prejudices from the right as from the left. Every movement is already a manifested action. How shall we leap over denials and cover the actions with something great enough?

The standard of beauty is not describable. It is a truism. To express one art by another is impossible. But we can take as basis some decisions to crystallize our feelings. And this thought triangle shall save us from difficulties in the judgments about beauty. Without spirituality, it is impossible to understand beauty; impossible to fly. Without experience, without love for knowledge, you can have no basis from which to start the ascent. Only without prejudice and conventionalities can you walk forward and grasp the rhythm of beauty.

There are many personalities, even specialists, with a great deal of experience but without the enlightenment of enthusiasm. For enthusiasm has its birthplace only in the beautiful land of spirituality. Very often one hears lectures devoted entirely to mechanical calculations, and how murderous they sound, these dead, dead signs. From these signs the consciousness becomes cold and weak, and they menace us as the greatest danger to the evolution of culture.

You have also sometimes seen how listless are the movements of the wings of spirituality without the muscles of personal experience. In distress, in pain, these lovely wings flutter, not knowing how to direct, how to verify their course. We must know where we are flying. Otherwise even the most mediocre, the most vulgar person, can hinder our path. And therefore, to know, to see, to hear the treasures of creation is so necessary.

Everyone is familiar with false spirituality, the conceit of little experience, the fetters of prejudicial chains. One may feel that a thought is ready to make its ascent, that its sails are full, that its rudder is already tested when suddenly an ill-smelling wind blows up from some small alley, and again dark prejudice flaunts itself and blocks the way to achievement.

Oh, human spirit, like a sponge you try to absorb all the obnoxious conventionalities of previous erratic lives. You hope to cure the old wounds with a plaster of vulgar consciousness. But with fetid rubbish you cannot fill up the crevices in the walls. The danger of miasma will penetrate the whole house. Now remark why people are so especially angry when you show them the real facts of their prejudices. Why is their spirit so indignant? Because you are touching the most vulnerable spot and for that reason, the influence of prejudice is so dangerous. The same microbes are found in palaces and in hovels, in universities and in temples.

You can purify your spirituality; you can garner experiences, but to watch the snarls and attacks of prejudices is extremely difficult. One may understand that the enlightenment of spirituality can come in a moment, when the ray of light touches a certain center. One can realize that experience cannot be collected so quickly, because even genius cannot so quickly assimilate the high pressure of new knowledge. But it is very difficult to conceive that even the vivid and brilliant brain is always in danger of a new paroxysm of prejudice. It is a special type of recurrent fever. And the one cure against this malady is the strong consciousness that you overcome the power of those microbes. Certainly you must not forget that the high point of this illness of prejudice is already incurable. And how many such incurable persons do we see! Eager to contaminate you with their illness.

For about thirty years I have had the experience of associating with youth with the help of art. Imagine how many judgments, how many combats I have met. But even among these people one can proclaim the above basis for the judgment of beauty. Let me repeat it: "Through intuition, on the basis of many personal experiences, without any conventionality or prejudice." On this basis, far-sightedness is transformed into creative clairvoyance. And with it, the enthusiasm of harmony can be attained.

I shall know! I can create! I am free!

New York, 1923.

CHAUVINISM

A FUNDAMENTAL kinship and similarity exists between America and Russia which will work for a close relation between the two countries. Before my departure to Asia, I am glad to speak about my belief in the future unity of the two nations:

Though my exhibition which has practically encircled this country, I have had the special opportunity of studying America, from many sides. I have visited the Middle West, California, New Mexico, Arizona, Maine—and all America's natural beauties are before my eyes.

I came to America not as a refugee, because no one expelled me from Russia. I came as a friend. Twenty-five years ago I appreciated America already, and assisted in bringing about closer relations between the two countries through Art. At that time it was only my intuition, but now it is knowledge and conviction, and I understand why these two countries have always had a peaceful entente and why the closest relationship between them is possible.

Not only in the greatness of Nature, in the immensity of their countries and in the variety of conditions, are these two peoples similar. Not only in the richness of their natural resources are they alike. But the general character of the peoples is also very close, one to the other.

An important condition allowing these similarities is that both countries are not so deep in prejudice and they both have so-called Open Eyes. The following particularly significant condition must not be forgotten: In Russia always, every foreigner was, is and shall be welcomed. The Moscow Kremlin was built by Italians. In some of Moscow's museums you see entire permanent collections of foreign artists. My own collection of paintings, which has been nationalized in the Hermitage (Petrograd), was composed entirely of foreign artists. In the government theatres there were always special Italian or French companies.

From the most ancient times in Russia this was so. Prince Vladimir the Saint invited to his country Byzantine artists. Prince Andrew invited Alani artists. The Moscovite Czars invited Italians. Peter the Great invited the Dutch. Catherine the Great invited many French artists, and afterwards, during the reigns of Alexander the First and Nicholas, we saw many German, French, and Italian artists. None of the foreigners were ever opposed. And their styles were all assimilated in a great creative combination.

In some small countries one often feels the presence of narrow chauvinism. And what small results issue from these petty countries. Chauvinism is the worst prejudice and from it have resulted wars, hatred and all struggles. And if we can have a world-feeling above this narrowness, we are already on the right path for the coming beautiful achievements. One can easily understand why America is so far from this narrow chauvinism. During one occasion in Chicago, I casually inquired how many nations there were together in the room and at once we found that there were fifteen nations together, discussing a subject of mutual interest. This meeting was dedicated to art and one has already heard many times that on this bridge of beauty can be united even the most diverse spirits.

Coming to America I felt that America, like Russia, was great because so many nations were assimilated here. During my two and a half years' stay not once have I felt the slightest opposition to the foreigner. And in this broad feeling is the best future. From this bright outlook is born the finest creative force. And only through creative work is the balance of a country established.

Amidst many ideals of unity and practical collaboration, I have seen how practically the idea of uniting all branches of art was spread throughout the United States. And really such an idea as the Master Institute of United Arts must be very near to the unifying spirit of America. Executives and advisors have sometimes whispered to me that people are as always very narrow and superficial. But I do not agree with them, because during my entire career of thirty years I have felt that the people as people are not stupid and that the essential feeling of the crowd is deep. But you must convince the crowd that you are sincere and then the most simple hearts are open. And who will build the future if not the newcomers, who take for their basis the synthesis of all previous experiences?

One very well-known American has told me that now he is addressing only children. Without exaggerating this idea, we can also point out that perhaps just now is the most propitious moment when the new generation must be addressed in the broadest way and must feel that all doors are open. And we must also understand how many doors heretofore have been closed. This searching without conventionalities or pigeon-hole prejudices will give to the country a wonderful future generation.

One may ask at what age we should begin to give the children genuine things. But really we should begin from the very first day. All falseness and especially all ugliness in children's literature must be purged and replaced by something true and deep. Before the children are spoiled, by intuition, they desire always to have in their hands some true objects. The things of the older generation always provide the best amusement for the children. And if we do not fear to give them the truth, really we can achieve.

Only let us repeat that we can know the happiest future by traversing the bridge of real beauty, without chauvinism or prejudice. On this bridge America and Russia shall be united.

Sincerely, I shall be so glad to return to America and see again my dear friends in this country.

New York, 1923.

THE RIGHT OF ENTRANCE

WINGS, Wings! You grow painfully. Beginning in 1914, humanity was plunged into cosmic upheavals. While some were occupied with evil destruction, others instinctively began to move. A strange phenomenon occurred: with the growth in the number of people killed, the number of travellers increased along all ways of communication. The apparent decrease in population had as its result the crowding of cities and hotels. Everyone rose up, everyone began to move. And like a sleepy man in a nightmare, the governments waved their hands trying to prevent the moving instinct of nations by putting petty difficulties of visas and special permissions in their way. But the human stream crashed all the barriers.

For nine years already, humanity has been wandering. They are hustling each other from one corner to another. The vocabulary of good and of abuse has been exhausted, and the earthly globe itself is becoming too small.

But amidst convulsions and dangerous experiments in search of the land of wonders, the wings begin to grow. Thoughts attain higher summits, and through the mist of dreamy visions, begins to glow the true possibility of attainments. Painfully the wings are growing.

Dear people, again I see in your hands Bædecker's guide-books containing full accounts of Beauty to be seen. Railways, hotels, Cook travel agencies and all institutions established for the travelling crowds are nourished through the martyrdom of Art and Knowledge. Dear people, you know well how to use the laboratory of creation, which does not belong to you. Even your eyes, blinded by the turmoil of life, are seeking a cure through the balm of Beauty.

By a tremendous effort, some have built the Pantheon of Beauty, and some have suffered to classify the achievements of research.

But here comes your motor car and an experienced cook offers you the "choicest food of Beauty." Can your stomach digest that food? And have you the right to enter the refectory? Have you ever produced anything that could justify your approach to art and knowledge? And in general, do you know how to give? And were you told that only those who give can receive?

But if you have no right to enter the temple, if you have not earned that right by your own labour, and if you only wish to be the receivers—are you not exposed to being called parasites? For you are simply crawling all over the temple adding nothing to it. You are furrowing the face of earth; you are impudently crowding the steps leading towards the achievements of others and foolishly believe that all creations and work are for you.

So be honest today and admit that not only have you done nothing for the progress of Art and Knowledge, but that you do not even know how to approach it! And how poor are your excuses!

At times, you listened to music, sometimes your eye wandered over paintings, your hand even tapped some sculptures, and yawning, you sacrificed an hour of your time to listen to a discourse by an eminent lecturer.

But after the motor car carried home your precious body, what was the result of your impressions? Boredom, yawning, dinner gossip and slander. Therefore, when a man rich and full of possibilities speaks to you about Art and Knowledge, always ask him: "What have you done for Beauty, that you should have the right to speak about it?" And besides that, you should tell him: "From this day on, seeing Beauty, you will always remember that you will remain a parasite, until you bring your stone for the building of the eternal Temple and until you earn the right to enter it."

We see some who have never sacrificed anything. We see men with dead expressions, painfully spending their time near salutary sources, waiting for their turn to swallow a draught of mechanical life. We hear their talk full of regret for yesterday. And the whole world is closed to them.

They cannot understand that their dullness would vanish quickly if only one of the eternal purposes of Beauty could be revealed to them. And they should understand that neither age, sickness nor prejudices should hinder them from approaching the eternal joy of spirit. For joy and not suffering was proclaimed!

What a painful sight to think of men aimlessly facilitating your aimless way! What a pity to think of your dressmakers and washerwomen! And sad for your drivers, for you do not even know what instructions to give them.— While close by lies the beautiful world, the world of joy, creations and achievements. For a caress, for a smile for Beauty, the key of the first Gate will turn. And for a desire to sacrifice, the bolt of the next Gate will fall.

Try to give something or at least offer something, but without selfishness and doubt. The reward a hundredfold greater is already awaiting you. And not in a future life, but right now here, if only you grasp the rhythm of life.

Rhythm is harmony. Travellers searching for the right of entrance know how to give!

"Thou who hast an ear,
Thou who hast an open eye,
Thou who perceivest me.
Be blessed.
Direct thine eye like a falcon into the distance,
Through Beauty shalt thou approach,
I bid thee pronounce Beauty!"

Vichy, 1923.

NEW ERA

GREAT changes have taken place during the last decade. Many walls of prejudice and of ignorance have been destroyed. The new forces coming into life are knocking at the door. Only the blind and deaf do not recognize it. And the coming of these new messengers is as simple as the coming of everything great always is.

Three gifts of perception are sent to humanity. The perception of One Spirit brings into being the unity of Love of Religions. The perception of the miracle of Art creates the realm of Beauty. The perception of cosmic force brings to us the idea of one universal Power. And in the name of the enlightened New Era, we have to accept these blissful gifts with prayers and in constant readiness for action.

The Inquisitors did not trust Galileo's statement on the revolving of the earthly globe. Solomon de Caus was placed in an insane asylum because of his belief in the power of steam.

Fulton was ridiculed even by his own brother. Galileo wrote with grief that professors in Padua refused to acknowledge anything concerning the planets, the moon and even the telescope, and that they were searching for truth neither in the world nor in nature, but by comparing texts and trying, by advancing logical proofs, to deprive the sky of planets.

Two hundred years later, Hegel, basing himself on philosophical proofs, tried to demonstrate the impossibility of the existence of planets between Jupiter and Mars. But in the very same year Piazzi discovered the first of the small planets.

Auguste Comte denied the possibility of analysing the

chemical nature of stars. Five years later, the inventors of spectral analysis established the classification of stars according to their chemical constituents.

Arago, Thiers, Proudhon were unable to foresee the future of railways. Thomas Joung and Fresnel were publicly ridiculed by Lord Broom because of their discovery of light-waves.

In 1878 Bouillot, Member of the Institute, witnessing the demonstration of Edison's phonograph by Demoncel before the French Academy, declared that this was only a trick, and six months later urged the Academy not to trust "American charlatans."

And not long ago the existence of America itself was denied.

So it was. So it is. But it shall not always be so.

"Judge by deeds only", "Judge only by results." Now in the time of action, not of discussion, let us remember this simple slogan. In our hard days of struggle and fight, humanity is growing weary of discussing all the conditional forms of contemporary life. But without a true conception of life proper, all the deliberations about its outward and casual signs are useless. You can talk about ways of communication, trade, production, monetary systems and innumerable related subjects. But where do we arrive with all these "ways of communication"? Are they, in the synthesis, going to serve us even as a means for murder? No, while there is no peace, the "ways of communication" are doomed to be broken up and all the products of man will be wiped from the face of the world. But there will be no peace until people learn how to discriminate between "mechanical civilisation" and the future culture of the spirit.

Even an approximate understanding of the fundamentals of true culture will create proper conditions for all the brilliant discoveries that are awaiting mankind in the near future. Much will be achieved if explorers, daring and confident, know how to approach the true nature of things without any prejudices, which are characteristic of merely outwardly-civilized people. Life is still full of prejudices seemingly fit only for the dark Middle Ages. However, there has never been so favorable a moment for the advent of genuine knowledge and beauty.

You can claim that the expression of individuality of the various peoples always takes a different form. But one condition will hold for ever: the forms of life must not only be civilized, but have the elements of culture. And when you discuss the future, have in mind the essential conditions, that it must rest within the bounds of true culture.

But how shall the conception of culture which is so easily understood, but not transmuted, be brought into life? Certainly not by words and proposals. What is needed now is harsh, practical and enlightened labor in its deep realistic meaning. The coming harvest of the forgotten forces of nature will blossom only in the soil of this reality.

Through creation and knowledge this reality of culture will take its place in life. Only great Beauty and Wisdom will strengthen the actual path of life. And now the time has arrived for concentrated work. And every worker should realize that he is not merely an insignificant part of a complicated apparatus, but that the highway of attainment lies open before him.

However, humanity is not erecting a polyglot Tower of Babel. The common language of mankind is known to everybody for whom Beauty is not a dead word. And the thoughts of it, pure as doves, fly the world around.

It is with special attention and great joy that we are watching the youth of today. Their hearts are sounding in a unique and quite new way. They are going to build the new world and when they are praised, our heart is filled with hope. And the praises are many, for youth is working and hence strengthening its spirit.

At this moment America is endeavoring to help many countries. This help makes us rejoice, for it comes from friends of the future. Those help who possess faith and clear foresight.

With hearts open to Beauty, encouraging young forces to a bright outlook, the people are deciding their future. During the present hard strife, the nations are beginning to understand why it is practical to retain the treasures of culture. They know that the new line should be erected according to these hieroglyphics of wisdom. Because the past is but a window to the future. Through this window will come the joy of presenting to friends the new peaceful discoveries of Beauty.

Many persons have asked me during this year what reason there has been for organizing now in New York the Master Institute of United Arts and Corona Mundi. Certainly to those who know the organizations there is nothing casual in their beginnings; they are answering the needs of our time. I was asked to state the missions of the two institutions and I chose two quotations from my articles, because in our day of keen struggle and international misunderstanding, I insist that they are purely practical.

For the Master Institute, I offered: "Art will unify all humanity. Art is one... Indivisible. Art has its many branches, yet all are one. Art is the manifestation of the coming synthesis. Art is for all. Everyone will enjoy true art. The gates of the "Sacred Source" must be wide open for everybody, and the light of art will influence many hearts with a new love. At first this feeling will be unconscious, but afterwards it will purify human consciousness. And how many young hearts are searching for something real and beautiful! So, give it to them. Bring art to the people, where it belongs. Not only museums, theatres, universities, public libraries, railway stations and hospitals, but even prisons should be decorated and beautified. Then we shall have no more prisons."

For Corona Mundi, the following: "Humanity is facing coming events of cosmic greatness. Humanity already realizes that all occurrences are not accidental. The time for the construction of future culture is at hand. Before our eyes the re-evaluation of values is being witnessed. Amidst ruins of valueless banknotes, mankind has found the real value of the world's significance. The values of great art are victoriously traversing all the storms of earthly commotions. Even the "earthly" people already understand the vital importance of active beauty, and when we proclaim: Love, Beauty and Action, we know verily, that we pronounce the formula of the international language. And this formula, which now belongs to the museum and the theater, must enter everyday life. The sign of beauty will open all sacred gates. Beneath the sign of beauty we walk joyfully. With beauty we conquer. Through beauty we pray. In beauty we are united. And now we affirm these words—not on the snowy heights, but amidst the turmoil of the city. And realizing the path of true reality, we greet with a happy smile the future."

Those who sit in pigeon holes may believe that these statements are too idealistic and can doubt their practical application in our day, amidst our complex life. But this doubt comes only from personalities who have limited knowledge, narrowed by the stress of urban life. Our way is not with these, for we have seen how the buildings of their limited knowledge are easily destroyed. But take the simpler souls, not from the dark city, but those closer to nature, from town and village, from that universe where the wings of possibility are growing. From these you will have an entirely different response. Even simple Russian peasants understood that in the art object was the real value, more stable, more firm, than in any pecuniary possessions. In the same way, these peasants felt the significance of music and song—and really, if serpents can be charmed with music, how much greater is its importance for the human soul?

Without any exaggeration, I emphasize that not one government can endure henceforth unless it takes into consideration the veneration of beauty expressed in all branches of art and higher knowledge.

And if the transports carry for trade, not guns, but beauty, one may believe that not one hand would be found to destroy these objects. There is one point at which beauty always conquers, when even the sceptical ones are confounded and begin to realize that they have to deal with something beyond themselves.

All the possibilities of the lower ways have already been tried. We have such superb poisons, and such all-destroying explosives, and our knives are so keenly sharpened that every heart can be destroyed. What a splendid apotheosis of destruction. We have had to reach the second thousandth year of our era to achieve such perfect enmity. And at the same time hypocrisy is at its flood tide. For we pretend great concern with international law. Pity the professor of international law, for his position now is very insecure; to discuss peace at a table beneath which is lying the most powerful explosive is hardly pleasant. And there is no rescue for them. No possibility of being saved until they have returned again to the right way.

Should someone wish to dispute with me this matter, denying the vital side of Beauty, I would gladly discuss it with him. I have on my side the soundest historical facts and what I am saying is based only upon results. When people accuse me of being only an idealist, I can well say: No, I am a realist because I believe in knowledge and facts, in the synthesis of beauty, while you base your faith on scraps of paper.

Nor, in speaking of art, do I refer necessarily to the great manifestations of art, to the Chaliapins, the Wagners. For them a small glimpse of sincerity possesses such mysterious conviction that in approaching it, you feel a breath of purer air. Recently at the Master Institute a very young boy gave his first recital, and one could perceive how, in hearing him, quite different hearts were united; even antagonists were for that moment in unity. If this principle is sound, certainly such a moment can be extended to infinity. And all difficult social and national problems can be solved in a moment because they do not exist in reality. Beneath this ascendancy of Beauty, you can distinguish the great visage of our religion, manifesting itself in the simplest way under the wings of beauty.

I believe always that the most idealistic ideas are the most practical, and so it has proved in every organization in which I have had the opportunity of participating during my artistic career. If anyone argues that something is too idealistic and hence outside of life itself, one can say. "Excuse me, you are wrong. It is out of life because it is not high enough. Compare it to mathematics where we have to deal with strange figures that do not seem to be vital, but in their application these figures become magnetic forces attracting life in all its atoms. And only in this way does one find the true ascent which leads us to the truism: from the highest mountain one attains the brightest outlook. And from the clearest outlook one can discern how the seeming destruction is in reality part of the great constructive work."

I have many friends among the children and I have always been especially proud of the little visitors to my exhibition. For who can grasp in the easiest way, the vital power of art?—The simple people and the children, the people of nature. In organizing the new international army of the new era, we must not forget the simple people and the children. The new era must have its new knights. And the best countersign of the army—the true passport for honor and eternity—is the sign of true culture. Before this countersign all communications shall be opened. And how simple and how beautiful shall be this vital sign.

We have noticed that the greatest enemies of Beauty are vulgarity, hypocrisy, selfishness, and above all, ignorance. The last one, although harmful, is not so dangerous. For this ailment may be cured, and my advice for finding a remedy is to go to the first sources; the sincere outlook, based on real facts, will open the eyes of those afflicted. One woman acquaintance, who lectures and sincerely attempts to interpret the meaning of art, once asked me what I would call her profession. I replied that the best title was probably "window cleaner." And this is not entirely jest. For I assert that every human being has an open view into this realm of Beauty if only the dust of life and the dirty windows do not obscure his vision.

I recall also another conversation with a man in an official position, who wanted to speak to me about this subject. During a conversation of three hours, he refused everything I told him and I accepted everything he told me. Finally I told him, "Now for the past three hours you have denied everything of mine, while I have found a place for everything you have said. Please comprehend whose position is better." And I saw how really amazed he was to realize that he was only a negative spirit. And how many of these opposing spirits in official life cross our path, always and only denying. But when their eyes are opened they will be astonished at their own bigotry. And they will see how easily, in our everyday life, a new order and a new realm can be established in the most vital way.

Remember not dreams, but facts. And results. And from where comes the most bracing energy to grasp the vital ideas. My friends, only from the infinite power of the air, of the sun, only from the light, comes this life-giving smile.

Monhegan, 1923.

"The evolution of the cosmos begins when I reflect My intelligence on the eternal energy."
Bhagavad Gita, Ch. III.

JOY OF ART

From a lecture given at California University, on September 19, 1921.

LITTLE knowledge brings darkness with it; great knowledge brings light. Spurious art brings the commonplace; genuine art creates joy of spirit and that power on which the building of our future rests.

We should now firmly establish everything that can lead Man along a new road. As in prehistoric times Paleolithic was replaced by Neolithic, so in our days the "mechanical civilization" is about to be replaced by the culture of spirit. The Druids secretly cherished the laws of wisdom; similarly, in the emerging kingdom of spirit, attention is tending towards knowledge and beauty, and many a home is already lighted up by that sacred fire; many are united, each of them a creative atom in the new construction. The same thought springs up in different countries simultaneously, like a strong plant sending forth many new shoots from the same root.

Friends, you would like to hear about art in Russia? You seem to be interested in it and kindly expectant. You are right. The Russian nation has always been closely attached to art. Since the times of yore all traditions have been permeated by true art. The ancient heroic epos, the folk-lore, the national string and wind instruments, lace, carved wood, ikons, ornamental details in architecture—all of these speak of genuine, natural artistic aspirations.

And, even at the present moment, all exhibitions, concerts, theatres and public lectures are invariably crowded. In Petersburg and Moscow, 5,000 people out of 2,000,000 inhabitants visit every exhibition (whereas, by the way, the same 5,000 are the average for visitors to an art exhibition in London out of her 10,000,000 inhabitants).

It was but a short while back that Kuprin wrote:

"Russian villages welcome intellectuals. They have become more in tune with the peasants' conception. A newcomer from among the students, man or woman, is trustfully asked to teach small village children, while their elder brothers and sisters are keen on learning not only music, but foreign languages as well. Wandering photographers are met with lots of orders. A painter who is able to produce on a piece of canvas or of linoleum an approximate likeness to a human face can be assured of a long life of security and comfort in the country. I say secure because the village bestows its sincere guardianship upon these artists."

I, too, could point out numberless instances of love of art and of enlightenment among the simple Russian people.

It would be impossible to cover in one article every section of the vast horizon commanded by Russian art. But it is possible to point out the milestones, and to map out the main roads which lead us from our day into the depth of the ages.

Besides admiring the modern Russian masters—Serov, Trubetzkoy, Vrubel, Somov, Bakst Grigoriev—you have shown your appreciation of our outstanding nationalists, such as Repin and Surikov, Nesterov and Levitan. You also recognize the names of old masters: the classic Brulov, the religious genius Ivanov, the interpreter of national life Venezianov, and our great portrait painters, Levitzky and Borovikovsky. But it is necessary all the same to point out the characteristic national features and movements of Russian art from a bird's eye point of view, as it were.

What shall we discard from our art in marking each

successive step of development? What shall we adopt? Which way shall we turn?—Towards the new interpretation of classicism, or to the antique sources? Shall we sink into the depths of primitivism, or find new light in "Neo-nationalism", with its fragrance of Indian herbs, its spells of the Finnish land, its inspiring thoughts of the so-called Slavophilism?

We are deeply excited over the question: From where is coming the Joy of Art?... For it is coming—although it has been less perceptible of late. Its resounding, approaching strides can already be heard.

Amongst recent achievements, one is notable and bright: the understanding of the decorative, of the adorning nature of art, is growing rapidly. The original purpose and meaning of art is again coming to the fore, rightly understood as the embellishment of life—which leads the artist and the on-looker, the master and the owner, to join in the ecstasy of creation and to exult in its enjoyment.

We have reason to hope that these modern aspirations will fling away the dead weights forcibly attached to art in the last century. Already the word "to adorn" seems to be acquiring its renewed meaning among the masses.

Very valuable is the fact that the cultured part of society is just now keen on studying the birth-springs of art: it is through these crystal-like springs that the understanding of the great value of embellishing human life will be reborn. It may acquire quite a new style and lead to a new era beyond the limits of our present imagination; but one thing is certain, that that new era in its intensity of exultation will be akin to the first human ecstasies.

But flowers do not grow on ice. In order to mold that new era it is necessary that society follow the artists; people should become their co-workers. The public mind, assisting art work by prompting its creations through the demand for exhibitions, art galleries and private collections, will be that warmth without which no roots can produce plants. Happily, as I say, everyone wants to see through the veil of the past, where the genuine gems are shining: either resplendent or humble, but equally great in the purity of thought that has given them their material form. We are trying to discern what we would see if we were transferred into the depth of those times: would we be amazed at the wisdom of an innate artistic instinct, or would we find just gifted children around us?—No, we would find not children, but wise men.

We are not going into the details of various ancient art creations: measurements and explanations might offend both their masters and their modern possessors. It is the impression of harmony that is essential in art; and what still bears the fascination of beauty and purity, of nobility and of singularity, should be counted as art, without needing to fear any libel. As it is, judging art creations of our day, many of us are apt to dwell on their flaws and drawbacks. This is a sign of the youth of a country where it is done.

Let us look at the Thirties of the last century and further back still. Much of it stirs our heart-strings: the noble bloom of the epoch of Alexander I, the truly decorative sparkle of the times of Catherine the Great and of Elizabeth XVIII, and the amazing creations of art in Peter the Great's time. Happily, a great deal of it has escaped ruin and vividly speaks for itself.

What is much less known and understood is the period before Peter. Our perception of these times has been out of gear for a long time due to the admixture of "self-made" knowledge—which is always the result of little knowledge. The safest way to study the homes and churches of the pre-Peter epoch is to transfer into them in our minds the treasures from our museums: jewelry, clothing, textiles, icons, etc.

Almost the highest place amongst the ancient Russian art creations should be given to the icons—applying this definition on a large scale. The faces on these "wonder-working" paintings are magically impressive. There is a great understanding of the effects of silhouette-painting in them, and a deep sense of proportion in the treatment of the backgrounds. The faces of Christ, of the Virgin, of some beloved Saints—they seem to actually radiate the power attributed to them: The Face of Judgment, The Face of Goodness, The Face of Joy, The Face of Sorrow, The Face of Mercy, The Face of Omnipotence... Yet—still The One Same Face, quiet in its features, fathomless in the depth of coloring: The Wonder-working Face.

Until recently, no one dared regard the icons purely from the point of view of pure beauty, and only now has a powerful decorative spirit been discovered in them—in place of the naivete and crudeness which were supposed to be their characteristics hitherto. A genuine decorative instinct gave their unknown creators, in their day, complete mastery even over the largest surfaces of church walls. We still cannot see the connection between this instinct and true technique and Knowledge, but the "specialists'" indifferent descriptions of these canvas-icons often call forth feelings of pain and offense with regard to those works.

Is it not sufficient to sense the exulting audacity of color in the wall paintings of the churches in Yaroslavl and Rostov?—Just have a good look at the interior of John the Baptist in Yaroslavl... What harmonies of the most transparent azure with bright ochre! What an atmosphere of ease and peace in the greyish emerald of the verdure, and how well it blends with the reddish and brownish ornaments of the figures. Serene Archangels with deep yellow haloes flying across the warm-looking sky—their white robes seeming only a shade colder against it. And the gold: it never hurts your eye, it is so perfectly placed and so perfectly balanced. Truly, these paintings are the daintiest, the finest silk, as befits the walls of the church of John the Baptist.

In the labyrinth of the church passages in Rostov every one of the tiny doorways startles you with an unexpected beauty of color harmonies. Softly-outlined human figures are discerned looking at you through the strangely transparent pale ash-grey of the walls. In some places you seem to feel the heat of the glowing red and chestnut tones;

in others, peace comes breathing from the greenish-blue masses of color; and, suddenly, you stop short—as before a severe word from the Scripture—faced by a shadowy figure in ochre.

You feel that all this has been created consciously, not casually; that you have been brought to that house of God for a reason, and that you will keep the impression of its beauty, taking lasting good from it.

These works—to quote from an old book of the XVIIth century—were painted "with honest mind and purpose, and with noble love for embellishment, for the people to see themselves here as standing before the face of The Highest."

When the later famous "wonder-working" icon of the Virgin Tverskaya was to be painted, the wood for its foundation was bathed in consecrated water, an exceptionally arduous service was held, the paints were mixed with the petrified remains of Saints, and the painter, while creating that work, consumed food only on Saturdays and on Sundays. The ecstasy of painting an icon was great in those days, and it was a real happiness when it fell to a true artist, elated by the eternal spiritual beauty which he was to embody.

Some splendid laws of the great Italians can be traced to the Russian wall paintings, applied from a purely decorative point of view. On the other hand, the Far East poured, through the Tartars, a tinge of willfulness into our old art works. As we approach the Tsarist period of our history (XVIth century), the decorative element in everyday life reached its highest point. Temples, palaces, or small private dwellings all clearly reflected a perfect sense of proportion through which the structure itself blended with its ornamentations into one. Looking at them you find nothing whatever to argue against.

The noble character of the arts that flourished in Novgorod and in Pskov—on "The Great Waterway" leading from the Baltic to the Black Sea—was saturated with the best elements of Hansa culture. The lion's head on the coins of the Novgorod Republic is very like the head of the lion of St. Mark... Was it not the northern giant's dream of the distant southern queen of the seas, Venice?... The now white-washed walls of Novgorod—the "Great Town which was its own Master", to quote its ancient name in full—look as if they could very likely have borne paintings in the Hansa style. Novgorod, famous for, and made wise by, the incessant raids of its "Freemen", might have hid from a casual wanderer its true form, not from shame, but from caprice: there is not one stain on the fame of the famous old town; it kept many of its old features even until the XIXth century.

It is different with the influences of the Far East. The Mongol invasions left such a hatred behind them that their artistic elements are always neglected. It is forgotten that the mysterious cradle of Asia produced these quaint people and enwrapped them in the gorgeous veils of China, Tibet and Hindustan. Russia not only suffered from the Tartar swords, but it also heard through their clashing the wonder-tales known to the clever Greeks and the intelligent Arabians who wandered along the Great Road from the Norman realms to the East.

The Mongol manuscripts and the annals of the foreign envoys of those days tell us of an unimaginable mixture of cruelty and refinement among the great nomads. The best artists and masters were to be found at the headquarters of the Tartar Khans.

Besides the adopted view-point of the textbooks, there can be another one:

It was the Tartars' contempt and cruelty that taught the Russian Princes to give up their feuds and to rally against their mutual oppressor; it was the Tartars that taught them the omnipotence of merciless victors; but, at the same time, those nomads brought from Asia ancient culture and spread it all over the land which they had previously devastated.

It is more painful to think of the ancient weapons of

the Russians themselves with which, in their quarrels, they ruined each other's towns, even before the Tartars invaded them. The white walls of the Russian churches and towers—"shining as white as cheese", to quote from the ancient annals—suffered many a hard blow from kindred clans.

Walking through the plains beyond the outskirts of Rome, one is unable to imagine that it was in those now empty places that Caesar's capital was developing, a marvel of shelter for some ten million inhabitants. It is equally unbelievable to imagine the splendor of Kiev—"The Mother of Russian Towns"—where Prince Yaroslav the Wise entertained foreign guests from East and West. The remnants of the wall paintings in Kiev's cathedrals, all these large-eyed, serene figures of worldly-wise men, interpreted by the brush of real artists, give us a glimpse of what art actually meant to the Russians of those times (about 1000-1200.)

A few years ago were excavated in Kiev some remnants of ancient walls, frescoes, tiles and ornaments; these are believed to be fragments of the Princes' Courtyards. I have seen some of the exquisite frescoes, and I found that they bore the features of the art of Asia Minor. The structure of the stone walls in itself indicates a special quaint technique, which usually marks the periods of great love for architecture. I think that the Rogère Palace in Palermo gives an idea of the palaces of Kiev.

It was really a combination of North and South: the metal sheen of the Scandinavian style, beaded with the pearls of Byzantium, made the ancient city that place of beauty which led brothers to fight for it. The astounding tones of enamel, the refinement of miniatures, the vastness and dignity of the temples, the wonders of metalwork, the mass of hand-woven textiles, the admixture of the finest laws in the Roman tradition—all these melted into one, to give Kiev its noble elegance. Men of Yaroslav's and Vladimir's times must have had a highly-developed sense of beauty, otherwise the things left by them would not have been so wonderful.

Note those paragraphs from the heroic epos where the people's mind dwells on the details of ordinary life, leaving for a while the achievements of heroism. Here is a description of a private house—a *terem*:

Around the terem—an iron fence;
Its spikes—topped with carving;
Each one of them crowned with a pearl.
The gateway—floored with whale tooth.
Over the gateway—about seventy ikons.
In the middle of the court—the terems rise,
The terems with their gilt domes;
The first doorway—in wrought iron work.
The middle doorway—in glass;
The third doorway—latticed.

One can trace in this description a similarity to the images on Aegean structures and Trojan columns.

And here is a description of horsemen:

Their clothes are of scarlet cloth.
Their leather belts are pierced with wrought metal
 clasps.
Their caps are black and pointed.
In black fur, with golden crowns.
Their feet are shod with precious green leather,
Shoes tilted at the toes like awls;
The heels are pointed too;
There's room enough for an egg to roll round the toes,
There's room enough for a sparrow to fly under the
 heels.

This is an exact, although poetic, description of the kind of garments that can be seen in Byzantine wall-paintings. And here again is the picture of the hero himself:

The helmet on his cap shines like fire.
His plaited shoes are in seven shades of silk.
Each has a golden tack in it;

On his shoulders—a coat of black ermine,
Of black ermine brought from over the seas,
Covered with embossed green velvet.
Each button-hole has a bird woven in,
And each golden button—a furious beast cast in.

I would suggest that we regard such a description not from the viewpoint of philological curiosity, but as a piece of direct realistic information. The details provide archaeologically true evidence. Thus, in this quaint statement we can see a fragment of a great culture,—one that was not enforced, not strange to the simple people: the unsophisticated folk, obviously, had no objection to it whatever: speaking of it without the scorn of the "lower" classes for "the elect", but freely expressing a genuine pride in what was beautiful and elegant to their own senses as well. In those days, the elaborate arrangements of the Princes' hunts, the merry feasts they gave—in the course of which they would put a number of wise questions before their foreign guests,—the nobility in the construction of new cities,—all this blended together in harmony. Such life did not jar on the poetic mind of the simple people; and it is evident that wise initiators of art inhabited and ruled The Mother of Russian Towns.

Here is a quotation from the first historical annals (the exact language of which remains untranslatable, being a mixture of Russian with the Old Slavonic, which in itself makes it a piece of poetry of the XIth century).

"Yaroslav founded Kiev the Great, and its Golden Gates with it. Also the Church of St Sophia, also the Church of the Annunciation upon the Golden Gates, also the Monastery of St. George and St. Irene.

"Loving the laws of Church and being a master in

books, he read them by day and by night, and wrote them too, thus sowing the written word in the hearts of true men, which we now reap. For books are rivers that carry wisdom throughout the world, and are as deep as rivers. Also, Yaroslav lovingly embellished the churches with gold and silver vessels, and his heart rejoiced upon it."

Yaroslav's exulting over the splendor of the church of St. Sophia is immeasurably removed from the exclamations of our contemporary savages at the sight of bright colors. Yaroslav's was the exultation of a man who sensed in his creation a monument of art that would live for ages. One can envy and admire the modes of life where such art was in demand.

A question may arise: How could Kiev have become a center of culture at the very start of Russian history?

Indeed, do we possess any knowledge about the foundation of Kiev?

That city tempted Prince Oleg the Varengian—a man of the world, a man of experience. Before him, the Princes Askold and Dir coveted Kiev, and so did many other Normans.—"And many Varengians foregathered and came into possession of the Slavonic Land."

It should be noted that there are no indications anywhere in the annals about Askold and Dir being un-cultured. Thus the facts about the foundation of Kiev are really pushed back into the depths of the legendary times. Let us not despise tradition, either; it says, for instance, that the Apostle Andrew visited Kiev; why should an Apostle come to virgin forests?—However, his appearance in Kiev becomes quite comprehensible if one thinks of the secret cults of Astarte which have been recently traced near Kiev. These cults take us back to XVI-XVIIth centuries B.C., when a large center of spiritual interest must have existed already in order to shelter such cults.

It is a comfort to know that all of the Great Kiev is still resting under the ground in peace, un-excavated. There are glorious discoveries to come yet. They will open almost the only gate into the depths of the past of our land. Even the Scandinavian period and the Bronze Age will have a light thrown on them through this gate.

There is no doubt that the joy of art grew in Kiev side by side with the neighboring Scandinavian culture, without in any way being created by the latter. Why should the birth of Russian Scandinavia be attributed entirely to the legendary Prince Rurik?—The ancient annals mention a fact which is of great significance, yet has never been picked up as a key:

"The Russians pushed the Varengians beyond the sea and would not pay duty to them."—Now, if the expulsion of the Varengians took place before Rurik's name was mentioned, when did their first appearance in the Russian land occur? It is quite possible that the Russo-Scandinavian era may have been rooted in the depths of the ages.

We have a startling illustration of carelessness in the "historical" text-books on the subject:

The famous phrase attributed to the old Russians, and given in the text-books as signifying a general invitation from the Russian land to the Varengians "from over the sea" runs thus:

"Our land is large and prolific, but there is no order in it. Come and rule over us." What is usually given as a sequence to this invitation are the following lines: "There came the Varengian Rurik with his brothers, Sineus and Truvor (862)."

Now, in the Scandinavian annals, the words *sin huus* and *truoer* mean, "his household" and "his true guard." Therefore I would suggest a different explanation of the famous phrase: very probable, it was uttered, not on the part of the ancient Russians themselves, but among the Scandinavian colonists who inhabited the banks of the northern river Volhov. It is they who must have asked Rurik from beyond Lake Ladoga (which is very much like a sea and where he, most likely, used to come from Scandinavia for hunting)—to come and organize a military force for them. And that man—with his household and his guards, with his means and his probable love of adventure—came at the request of his compatriots. By and by, his kind of "princes", warriors hired in the North of Russia, were attracted by the Kiev Principality, where the role of a "prince" was more than that of a warrior and included the position of statesman.

In the Xth century, northern culture saturated the whole of Europe with its influence. No one denies that the Scandinavian epoch poses one of the most attractive artistic problems. The monumental art of the Scandinavians is exceptionally serene and noble. For a long time it was only the skiffs with their motley sails and carved dragons that brought the elements of The Wonderful with them into Russia. Our people adopted these with open hearts. There is no reason to regard the Northerners as savage conquerors of the original Novgorod; in any case, they lived long and in a way that makes it clear that they knew true art—a feature which was a powerful factor in their blending with the inhabitants of the Russian plains, who had innate artistic imagination..

We know that the Varengians brought with them the idea of human deities: but, before that, did the Slavs not deify the powers of nature—one of the most poetic forms of religion? This was the cradle of their creative inspirations.

Going further into the depths of the ages, we find the last frontier of realistic entities. Apparently, only dust seems to be left beyond those frontiers, and an amateur is put hard to believe that it is not merely a theory of dull archaeology that we are asked to adopt. In reality, there indeed survived some atoms of fascinating splendor that did live in the past. Now it is time for everyone to realize that art has existed not only where this is obvious to all; but that much, much is hidden from us by the veils of time. And what seems dull now will appear one day lit up by the joys of discernment. The onlooker will become a creator. Herein lies the fascination both of the Past and of the Future. He who cannot grasp the Past is unable to imagine the Future.

The fantastic bas-reliefs on the northern rocks, the tall hillocks along the trade-routes, the long daggers and the attire so rich in design make one love northern life; they awaken respect for the primitive forms of beauty beyond which our imagination sinks in the depths of the bronze patinas.

A great deal of art can be sensed even in the far-off mysterious periods, so indistinct. Can the Finnish animal phantasmagoria be a stranger to art? Do the enchanted forms of the Far East escape artistic explanation? Are the first adaptations from the antique world hideous in the hands of the Scythians? Are the ornaments of the Siberian nomads merely coarse?

No: these finds are kindred to art, and one can envy the clarity of conception shown by the ancients. They incarnated symbols that meant to them so much, and created well-defined, distinct, manifold artistic forms.

It is in the mysterious cobweb of the Bronze Age that we have to search. Every day brings with it new conclusions. We can discern a whole pageant of peoples... Beyond the shining, gold-clad Byzantines we see the motley crowds of Finno-Turks pass by. Deeper still in time majestically come the splendid Aryans. Still deeper, there are only the extinguished bonfires of unknown wanderers; these are numberless...

It is the gifts which all of these have left for us that are nowadays building up Neo-nationalism. The younger generations will heed it and will become strong and healthy through it. If the blunted modern nationalism of art is to be turned into a bewitching neo-nationalism, the foundation stone of the latter will be the great ancient world in its genuine conceptions of truth and beauty. This truth and beauty will one day find its equal in the great future.

The remotest Russian annals of the Christian era are unable to convey the fascination of the effaced cult of Nature. The so-called "animal" in everyday life, the "devilish" in merrymaking, the "unseemly" song described by the chronicler of the ancient times—should not be swallowed wholesale as such: the chronicler was an ordained churchman, and a partial point of view was unavoidable in his case. The Church did not bring art with it; it only rested its foundation upon it, and, although it created some new forms, it crushed other, equally beautiful, ones.

All certainty of assertion ends for us with the Scandinavian period. What remains of the ages that preceded it gives us but approximate indications. We can only know that objects of beauty were necessary in people's lives; but what life was like, what art objects were in demand, and how these people believed in art, this we do not know.

Four and a half thousand years before our era, Babylonian culture was in full bloom. We know some stray characters, but to turn them into a fairy tale, let the specialists attempt this.

The darkling depths of the Bronze and Copper Ages are impenetrable for us, especially if we try to limit ourselves to the Russian milieu. Yet, such countries as Greece and Phoenicia were bound to have made an immense impression on the surrounding populations. Of course, the transitory moments of history must have effaced the importance of ornamental art even then, as also happened in Russia at the period of the internal feuds. The unskilled use of a new treasure such as metal must have pushed aside, at the time, real artistic taste. But the dark Ages of iron, bronze and copper lasted a very long time, and we cannot expect any clarity from our researches there.

Regarding ornaments, the creative spirit of the ancients worked unfailingly. The love for symbolic design enveloped humanity like a safety net; and a modern uncultured woman of the tribes of Mordva or Cheremissy (in the East of Russia) has no conception of the value of the art which has reached her through the ages and which she possesses in her ornaments.

San Francisco, 1921.

THE STONE AGE

HERE ends the standardization of life through metal. Here ends nationality and the conventions of political economy; here ends the role of the masses. Art alone does not end. A different man stands out clearly: it is from the Stone Age that he is looking at us. Joy of art has been rolling its waves through all the periods of life. The abyss between those waves has been very deep at times, but higher rose the crests of the waves so high, indeed, that we can discern them from our viewpoint.

Let some people look askance at the "deadness" of archaeology, and draw a sharp line between it and art. Even a self-denying lover can be excused his involuntary shudder as he approaches the Stone Age: for that age is too far from our modern conception of life—which makes it as difficult to grasp the realities of the Stone Age as it would be to see the depths of the firmament with a naked eye.

Humanity knew the joy of art, and we can still trace it. Let us forget for a while the sheen of metal. Let us think of the many wonderful shades of stone, of the noble hues of precious fur, the graining of self-colored wood, the yellow reeds and rushes, and the beauty of the strong human body of the cave-man. We should keep them in mind all the time while we try to penetrate into the atmosphere of the days when that man lived. Can we actually catch glimpses of it, and hear its echoes? Or, is it just possible to find a correct viewpoint?

The tradition of a Mordva tribe tells:

"The goddess Angi-Pattey, in her wrath, struck a flint stone against a rock,—and gods of earth and water, of forests and dwellings, appeared from the sparks. She finished with the flint stone and flung it to the earth: but it became a god too, for she had not killed the creative power in it. And the flint stone became the god of propagation. That is why a little hole in every yard, or under the threshold, is covered with a little flint stone god."

Let us compare this legend to the Mexican one:

"In the Mexican sky there were once upon a time the god Zitlal Tonnack, a shining star, and the goddess Zitlal Kuhe—the one that wears a starry garment. That starry goddess bore him a strange creature—a flint stone knife. Their other children, astounded, flung it down to earth. In striking, the flint stone broke into fragments, and one thousand six hundred gods and goddesses appeared from among the sparks."

Thus we see that the cosmogony of Erzia[4] is no poorer than that of the Mexicans.

"With a stone knife thou shalt kill the calf", orders the sacrificial ritual of Voti.

"The arrow sent by thunder lessens the pain in childbirth", is the belief among the unsophisticated Russian "healers."

"The Giants have buried a stone in the forests", remembers the progeny of Yem and Viess.

There are many more traditions and legends.

Each tribe has kept until now the mysterious foundation stone of the Stone Age. Customs and beliefs, as well as the half-legible materials of the ornaments, never give up the tale of the "pre-historic" times.

So are those times called; but they are not absolutely detached from ours: on the contrary, they find their way into the pages of our history. Where are the limits of life beyond which we can see no metals?

We Russians are in the habit of searching for the roots of our art very far back: We refer to India, Mongolia, China or Scandinavia, or to the grotesque imagination of the Finns. Yet, besides the impressions left by later tides, we

---

4 Mordva, Erzia, Voti, Yem, Viess are Finno-Slavonic tribes.

have, like every other nationality, the general human path leading back to the most ancient international hieroglyphics which explain the human love of beauty: this is the path through the Stone Age.

It can be foretold that, seeking for a more perfect existence, humanity will think more than once of the Free Man of ancient times. He knew Nature, and lived heart to heart with it, hand in hand. This is something that we have lost.

Harmonious were the motions of ancient man; sensible were his thoughts; he was exacting in his sense of proportion and in his love for ornamentation. It is a mistake, due to scanty knowledge, to define the ancient Stone Age as an era of the primitive, the utterly uncultured man. There are no traces of animal primitiveness in the stone pages that have reached us. We can only guess in them at the existence of a culture distant from ours, so distant, indeed, that we can hardly think of it as of a culture: it is too different from our erroneous conceptions of a "savage."

The now almost extinct uncultured natives with their flint stone spears resemble the man of the Stone Age just as much as an idiot resembles a sage: they are only degenerates, a few resemblances remaining as the only link left between those two. In reality, the man of the Stone Age set the birth-springs of all cultures to come. He had the power to do it; while a savage of our day has lost all his power over Nature—and with it all his sensing of her beauty.

Human existence, fighting and erring in its constant fear, has made a maze of itself; and, in order to see new open roads, we should discover those from where we started.

It is only recently that we have grasped that the entrance halls of the museums filled with dusty old metal illustrate, not a dark spot on the geological tree of our art, but its brightest shoots. This should command as much awe as does the fact that humanity has been in existence scores of thousands of years.

We are not deceived by the few fragments of bronze

and by the piles of crushed stone that are the only things found in the places where the main squares of immense cities stood once upon a time; we realize the smile with which Time has been playing. Just in the same way the Stone Age could not possibly be represented by the few fragments of stone that have remained on the surface of the earth.

Mystery dwells round the traces of the Stone Age. Its remains are attributed to a heavenly origin. Many gods are supposed to have sent their spears and arrows flying about the earth.

In the so-called Classical Era, the real derivation of the stone weapons could not be solved, and the Mediaeval Era failed in that task too. It was only towards the end of the XVIIIth century that some of the learned researchers succeeded in disclosing the origin of the most ancient objects made by man. But even their statements are scanty and vague. There are but a few of them that carry conviction; most of them still remain open to argument. This is not surprising because, if the lapse of just one thousand years makes it difficult to find an absolute definition with regard to some particular century—how much more difficult is it when scores of thousands of years have gone by? Even the Ice Age has been replaced in some of the theories by a sudden cosmic catastrophe.

Let us remember that all the names of the ancient eras have been given to them only "conditionally" and have come from the names of the districts where the ancient objects were found. One can imagine what wealth of unexpected things is still hidden within the earth, and what changes may be coming in the now established theories.

There have already occurred some startling instances of this kind. It is dangerous to associate scientific theories to our knowledge of ancient stone objects. The artistic point of view alone is possible. The investigations of the beauty of ancient life cannot impede the scientific proofs which will follow.

It is quaint that the aspirations of the Stone Age seem

to be the nearest to our modern search for beauty. The cycle of culture is but leading us back to what ancient man realized in his time: I mean the longing for harmony. The painful searching for the latter in our modern art particularly reminds us of the care with which ancient man tried to make his surroundings sensible and harmonious, embellished by his loving touch.

Each single object in our life gives an idea of its other ingredients. The excellent point of a spear tells of a handle that must have matched it. The same refers to any tool or weapon. The imprints of cords and nettings are very eloquent. It is obvious that home life with a cave-man had its fixed standard of comfort and beauty.

The breath of the Stone Age reaches us as a breath of the Joy of life. The hungry, greedy human wolves came but later on: Stone Age man was more like the king of the forests—the bear: satisfied with ample food, homely, powerful but good-natured, heavy but quick, furious yet kind, persevering yet benevolent. Such was the type of the Stone Age man.

Many of the peoples have the legend about the bear being "a man turned round." There exists quite a cult founded on this belief, because humanity senses in the bear many features akin to the first forms of human life. The cave-man is monogamist by nature; it is only the growth of the family—its capacity for work—that makes him stoop to polygamy. He values bearing children as a means to continue his creative work; he has a personal longing to create and to embellish things. The need of exchange, the habit of smartness and the fear of solitude appeared only in the later stages of human life. The cave-man admitted the social principles only where intermingling with others did not really affect his inner sense of personal freedom,—for instance, in hunting, in fishing.

The remnants of the first two epochs (as these are accepted by the geologists)—i.e. the petrified bones of the terrifying creatures that lived then—form a canvas for a boundless tale of imagination; but let us leave them to an artist's soul, to which they are as precious as the works of human hands. Let us also leave alone the third Pliocene with its mysterious forerunner of man. This is an area of guesses and inventions. The scratches found on petrified bones and on flint stones are not sufficient for substantive artistic evaluation. But the Chellian, the Acheulean and the Mousterian epochs of the Pre-Ice Age already approach art. We see man as the king of nature at that time. He has hand-to-hand fights with monsters; with assured blows he creates the wedge—his first weapon sharpened on both edges. The mammoth, the rhinoceros, the elephant, the bear, the gigantic deer yield to him their skins.

He leaves his dwelling, the cave, to the lion and the bear, and does not mind their being his neighbors, since he already protects his new dwelling with stakes. Another method of conquest occurs to him—he tames the beasts! This was an exciting time of numberless conquests.

Then we see man intuitively moved by the instincts of harmony and rhythm. In the two last epochs of the Paleolithic (Solutrean and Magdalenian) we see his dwelling and his home life perfected by means of art. All that a solitary creature could make was created by the ancient man of that period.

The herds of deer provided him with excellent material for practical use. Man began making arrows, needles, ornaments, handles, etc., using deer horns. The first horn sculpture and the first designs belong to that period, also the famous little figure of a woman: the stone Venus of Brassempouy.

Various ornamentations were traced within the caves; their ceilings bear designs representing animals, and it is quite obvious that the artist of those days had an acute sense of observation and could convey the exactness of movement. The ease and freedom of his lines approach in their harmony the best Japanese drawings.

The caves in the South indicate beyond any doubt the true sense of art in ancient man; they bear traces of the first mineral paints and sometimes have complex designs on their ceilings. We may be certain that such dwellings were lit by hanging lamps, especially as the discovered objects of that period have high qualities of jewelry: the finest needles, bridles for deer, ornaments made of pierced sea-shells and of the teeth of animals.

As the principle of exchange was gradually taking root in man's mind, the power of imagination in producing desirable objects was bound to develop.

There is a break between the Paleolithic and Neolithic periods, which, to our minds, is filled with mystery. There might have been some cosmic changes, or different tribes of humanity came into existence, or, again, the cycle of a certain ancient culture might have come to its closing point; but the features of human life that can be distinctly traced next are different. Apparently, solitude lost its fascination for the mind of man. He had learned the charms of sociability. Creative interests become more versatile, then the treasures of spiritual maturity, accumulated by the solitary predecessors, lead to new achievements! New challenges are dealt with by new methods. Many skulls of that period are found to have been fractured with heavy weapons. Thus the man of the Diluvian (Quaternary) period entered the battle of life, which expressed itself in Neolithic.

In Russia, nothing striking has been found as yet illustrating our Paleolithic epoch: but Russian Neolithic is certainly abundant in the quantity and variety of its objects of art. All the best types of weapons can be found dating from this period.

The amber ornaments found together with flint stone work in the Baltic region belong to the period around 2000 B.C. Near Kiev a mysterious religious tribe appears not only to have possessed polished weapons in their place of worship, but also little statuettes of women which indicate their derivation from the cult of Astarte (XVI—XVIIth centuries B.C.).

At the battle of Marathon some of the units were using

flint stone arrows. All this shows how the periods of various cultures have overlapped each other.

From the Russian Neolithic we have found piles of weapons and of pottery on the banks of rivers and lakes. Putting together the fragments and following the re-appearing forms and designs, one feels amazed at the power of imagination reflected in them. Particularly characteristic are the remnants of pottery. They indicate that similar ornamentation was applied to clothes, to wooden dwellings, and to the human body itself: to all that could not outlive the pressure of time.

The same type of ornaments found their way into the epochs of metal; and even modern embroideries take us back to the most ancient era. For instance, the popular design of the deer has nothing to do with the polar regions unknown to the central Russian, but should be attributed to the times before the deer migrated to the far North, because the bones of that animal are found in abundance amongst the flint stones in the center of Russia.

The clay beads of the Stone Age often bear the design of a serpent—like the most ancient objects of the Aetian culture.

No reasoning against the innate instinct for art can withstand the facts: Is the nature of ornaments not the same for all people and all tribes, however isolated from each other by time and space?

The problem of the origin of ornamental art, in any case, leads us back to the primitive touches produced by primitive man: a hollow and a line. It is on these two elements that all ornamentation is founded. Ancient man, busy with molding huge boilers with rounded bottoms, or with making a tiny cup covered with a network of lines, was instinctively applying all the tools he could find: his hands, his nails, quills, stones from meteoric showers, strings, nets. Everyone tried to make the vessels of his household as valuable and beautiful as he could.

One can sense the keenness of the cave-man in covering the whole surface of a boiler with tiny little holes or with interlacing designs. One can follow his excitement as an artist at the time when he first thought of applying strings, nets, even his own clothing, in order to leave the imprint of their material on the soft surface of the clay. But this also failed to satisfy him, and he discovered some vegetable paints and applied them eagerly. It is easy to imagine how many of his inventions must still be buried in the earth, or have been effaced by time, or by water; most likely the same red, black, grey and yellow tinges had been embellishing his clothes, his hair, even, perhaps, his body. Really, the fact that the cave-man did everything to embellish his surroundings stands out as a living reproach to us. There can be no comparison between our aspiration for art and his, who walked the same ground thousands and thousands of years ago.

Those who see ancient stone articles only behind the glass of museum cases can hardly avoid the error of feeling prejudice against their beauty. But take any original piece of a stone weapon and put it side by side with your favorite modern art objects: to your surprise, it will not bring any discord with it. Indeed, instead of jarring on you, it will add a note of nobility and restfulness.

If you wish to see the soul of an ancient piece of stone work, try to find one somewhere yourself. At first, you may not notice at all that you were lucky; but, in twisting it round in your hands, you place your fingers in the hollows originally meant for a similar human hand, and—from under the layers of age (which makes the stones grow grey too)—you will suddenly behold a beautiful work of love and beauty in a piece of jasper or of dark green jade.

The variety of tools, instruments and weapons fashioned by the ancients is much greater than is usually known. The Russian Neolithic proves this amply. There are so many complex objects amongst its remnants that defy, so far, our imagination as to their use.

It gives a feeling of satisfaction that praise is not merely heard in one's own country: at the Prehistoric Congress held in Perigueux in 1905, the best French connoisseurs,

Mortillet, Riviere de Precour, Cartailhac and Capitan hailed the exponents of the Russian Neolithic with enthusiasm, and placed the objects on the level of the Egyptian samples.

Are we able to picture in our minds the dwelling of a Stone Age man? There is no answer to that yet. But the fact we should bear in mind is, that often nothing is left but a heap of brown stone, even in the place of a very large building.

The remnants of pile dwellings indicate well-developed forms of home life. We certainly had them in Russia. It was an old idea with the Slavs to isolate their dwellings from the ground and to place them on piles. The little bungalows of this kind where the Siberian and Ural hunters to this day store away the skins of killed animals have lived through countless centuries. At the beginnings of trade, such stores played a significant part. Our first chronicler, Nestor, mentions "burials on piles or stakes by the roadside"; this refers to the ancient "huts of death", or, actually, isolated little tombs in the shape of little hog-huts on stakes. The favorite item of Russian fairy-tales, "the hut on chicken legs", is of the same origin. The existence of numerous islands on our broad lakes and rivers fostered the popularity of such dwellings which constituted whole villages.

Let us look just once more at the picture of life as it must have been in the far vistas of the Stone Age.

I can see a lake. A row of dwellings along its bank. There is something refined about their ornamentation which reminds you of India and Japan. There is harmony in the great gradation of color of stones, furs, wicker-work, pottery, and the tawny human skin itself. The roofs topped by tall chimneys are covered with dark yellow reeds and animal skins, and with some extraordinary net-work interwoven with thatch. The ridges are fastened together with carved planks of wood. Keepsakes of successful hunting are also used as ornaments over the corners of the roofs. Invariably there is the glaring-white horse skull that guards the place from the "evil eye." The walls of the houses are covered with ornamental designs in yellow, red, white and black. Inside and outside the dwellings, there are fire-places for bonfires, and above them vessels are suspended— beautiful ornamental vessels in brown and greyish-black. There are skiffs and nets at the water-side, fine, well-made nets. Animal skins are spread about to dry: bears, wolves, foxes, beavers, sables, ermine.

There is merry-making. A festival is taking place to hail the victory of the Spring Sun. The people have been in the forest and enjoyed the first foliage, blooms and grass, and have made wreaths of it all to wear on their heads. Quick, alert dancing is going on, to the piping of wood and horn-pipes. Many of the varied garments seen amid the crowd are trimmed with fur and with touches of colored needle-work. Smartly shod in leather and in woven footwear the people tread daintily. The younger merrymakers, forming rings for dancing and singing, wear amber ornaments, embroidery, stone beads and talisman teeth.

These people liked to please each other! These people throbbed with joy! Art already played a great part in it. They also sang, so that one could hear their blending voices far beyond the lake and forest.

The huge bonfires looked like living creatures of gold in the approaching dusk. The people's figures moved against them—quick or pensive, but filled with the sense of appreciation of life.

The water in the huge lake that looked stormy in the daytime now became peaceful and was like lilac-colored steel. Skiffs, taking their part in the festival, swiftly glided over it late into the night.

The Yakuts in Siberia, whose language has all but died out by this time, used to sing not so many years ago their ancient, ancient song of the spring festival; here is its literal translation.

"Hail, ye lush green hills! The spring warmth is reveling! The silver birch is unfurling! The smooth fir is brighter! The grass is green down in the glen! This is the time for games and for merry-making!

"The cuckoo is calling, the dove is cooing, the eagle is screeching, the lark is gone up to the skies, the wild geese are flying in pairs, birds with motley feathers have come back, and those with tufts are crowding together!

"Ye people who find your market in the dense forest—and your city amid the naked branches—and your street along the waterway!—whose prince is the woodpecker, and whose alderman is the blackbird! All of ye—speak out! Make your youth come back to you, sing without halting!"

The day will come yet when we shall learn much about the Stone Age. We shall appreciate that age and learn a lot from it too. Only the Indian and the Shaman wisdom has kept some reminiscences of it.

Nature will prompt us to grasp many mysteries of the beginning of things. But there will be no words to prompt us: there is no language left of those times; and no finds, nor fantasies, will lead us to it. We shall never know the song composed by ancient man. What was his shout of hunting, of wrath, of attack, of victory? What words did he use when reveling in his art? His word is dead forever.

The Mayan wise men have left an inscription. It is 3,000 years old, and reads thus:

"O Thou who wilt show thy face here after us! If thy mind thinketh, thou shalt ask—Who were we?

– Ask the dawn about it, ask the forest, ask the wave, ask the storm, ask love! Ask Earth—the beloved Earth filled with suffering!

– Who are we?

– We are Earth."

When ancient man felt the approach of death he thought with great calm:

"I am going to rest."

We do not know how they spoke in those days, but they thought in terms of beauty.

So we have traced man's love of art back to the Stone Age. You can see that our way was not inconsequential or casual; it has actually led us to the origins of real art and real aspirations for knowledge. And now I address you from the depth of the ages: you, the most modern people, and you who have lived through scores of thousands of years, and you, the conquerors of the globe.

Remembering all the great conquests of art, we should once again think of applying to real life the beneficent charms of beauty. Otherwise, materialism, in its last spasms, will threaten to choke the enthusiasm and spirituality that are awakening at the present time.

We may hear the complaints: "Beauty is becoming rare in our life. Single beautiful objects can be found but far apart, and they are unable to transform the sordidness of our existence. Great Pan is dead."

In the spheres of art one confronts hypocrisy more frequently than elsewhere. How many people use "high words" to talk about art and at the same time avoid it in their lives.

On the other hand, we can rejoice at the fact that many women and many of our younger generation are holding the torch of art on high.

We must not be sad. We must meet the cosmic phenomena with smiling gladness because we are now constructing new forms of life. We know by this time that art is placed as a foundation stone of every genuine culture. Humanity is beginning to understand again that creative work is not an unnecessary luxury. It is gradually recognized as a vital factor of daily life. We know that all aspects of life are set in motion only by art, by achievement of perfection in its manifold facets.

The world of Eternity illuminates our dark existence by the breath of its beauty; and we must walk the rising road of grandeur, enthusiasm and achievement with all the powers of our spirit. The new world is coming.

www.ingramcontent.com/pod-product-compliance
Ingram Content Group UK Ltd.
Pitfield, Milton Keynes, MK11 3LW, UK
UKHW020224250726
13967UKWH00001B/169

9 781947 016095